M000004361

FAITHFUL
Celebrations

MAKING TIME FOR GOD IN WINTER

Edited by

SHARON ELY PEARSON

CHURCH
PUBLISHING
INCORPORATED

Scripture texts referred to in this work are taken from the *New Revised Standard Version Bible*, copyright © 1989 by the Division of Christian Education of the National Council of Churches of Christ in the USA, and are used by permission.

Acknowledgments: Faithful Celebrations is the work of many unnamed contributors, as well as Carolyn Chilton, Janie Stevens, Dina Strong, Sylvia DeVillers, Sara Fontana, Kathy Finely, Rita Mailander, Kathy Coffey, Dirk deVries, Sharon Ely Pearson, and Jim Wahler.

Illustrators: Sally Brewer Lawrence, Anne Kosel, Victoria Bergesen, Tom Lybeck, and Paula Becker

Church Publishing
19 East 34th Street
New York, NY 10016
www.churchpublishing.org

Cover design by Jennifer Kopec, 2Pug Design
Typeset by Rose Design

Library of Congress Cataloging-in-Publication Data

Names: Pearson, Sharon Ely, editor.
Title: Faithful celebrations : making time for God in winter / edited by
  Sharon Ely Pearson.
Description: New York, NY : Church Publishing, [2018] | Includes
  bibliographical references.
Identifiers: LCCN 2018018461 (print) | LCCN 2018032939 (ebook) | ISBN
  9781640650961 (ebook) | ISBN 9781640650954 (pbk.)
Subjects: LCSH: Winter--Religious aspects--Christianity. |
  Holidays--Religious aspects--Christianity.
Classification: LCC BV135.W56 (ebook) | LCC BV135.W56 F35 2018 (print) | DDC
  263/.97--dc23
LC record available at https://lccn.loc.gov/2018018461

ISBN-13: 978-1-64065-095-4 (pbk.)
ISBN-13: 978-1-64065-096-1 (ebook)

Printed in Canada

Contents

Introduction

But speaking the truth in love, we must grow up in every way into him who is the head, into Christ, from whom the whole body, joined and knit together by every ligament with which it is equipped, as each part is working properly, promotes the body's growth in building itself up in love.

—Ephesians 4:15–16

In a small way, this book's intention is to help the Body of Christ grow in understanding and "build itself up through love" at church or home. Celebrations, gatherings, and rituals help members of every generation find both individual meaning and common ground, all through the medium of direct experience, no matter the age of the participant. *Faithful Celebrations: Making Time for God in Winter* offers a multitude of ideas for planning an event focused on a secular day that occurs during the winter months (in the northern hemisphere) that will bring families together and build strong communities of faith, whether it is in the home or a congregational setting. Since family relationships and community togetherness occur both inside and outside of a church setting, the celebrations within these pages come from secular or popular culture roots as opposed to religious seasons and holidays. These are offered from the perspective of, "How does this occasion relate to my Christian faith?"

Through such occasions we can become better acquainted with our extended family—young and old together—in any setting. We can take steps toward making our congregation (or neighborhood) the warm, nurturing community we long for in our fragmented world. Older adults sometimes feel a sense of displacement in congregational life today, and younger people are increasingly looking to a variety of sources for spiritual nurture and faith practice. Singing, praying, eating, and creating memories together enhances our well-being and makes our connections to one another stronger. Undergirding our experiences is the presence of God among us, nurturing us and working through us to help us grow in the knowledge and love of Christ Jesus.

Through community celebrations, we can experience scripture and traditions in a fresh way that can give beauty and meaning to our daily lives. Within these pages you will find ideas to hold a theme-based event, or simply ideas to supplement other activities you have planned. This abundance allows you to choose only those activities that meet your congregation's or family's particular needs—and fit your timeframe. *Faithful Celebrations* will help you and your family—at home, school, or church—learn more and experience these particular winter seasons:

- New Year's Day
- Martin Luther King Jr. Day (This is observed on the third Monday of January every year, coinciding with his birth on January 15. On the Christian calendar, he is recognized on April 4, the day he was martyred.)
- Super Bowl Sunday
- Valentine's Day
- Snow Days

ALL AGES GROWING TOGETHER

Many of the formative experiences in life happen when several generations are together. In our society we tend to separate people by ages mainly for education and employment. In recent years, Christian formation programs have made this same separation of generations, but more and more religious educators are recommending programs in which adults and children learn together. It is a way to pass on faith—generation to generation. Old learn from young, and young learn from old.

Faithful Celebrations is designed to meet the need for generations to learn together. This approach requires that we venture beyond traditional learning methods into the world of experiential learning. Just as old and young alike can participate in vacations, trips, holidays, and family events together, learning more about our relationship with God can take place with all generations growing together. This may mean that adults work alongside children, helping them as well as listening to them as full partners in an activity or discussion. It means allowing children to experience things for themselves, not doing things for them but with them.

WHEN, WHERE, WHY, AND HOW

Finding time and resources to add another component to already full schedules, both in families and in congregations, can be a challenge. Within your community of faith, look to different groups who could successfully host an intergenerational gathering. One promising lead might be to invite your youth organization to be in charge of leading one or more sessions. Consider also the possibility of asking different congregational organizations to host a given session. In a typical community of faith, consider using these ideas as:

- intergenerational and multi-age programming
- seasonal church gatherings for families
- primary Christian education material for a small church
- supplementary material for large Christian education programs
- supplementary material for classes in church-based schools
- home study Christian education programs
- small-community or base-community Christian education
- supplementary material for family sacramental programs

In a home setting, families can use these activities for:

- family vacations and holidays
- neighborhood or community events

- home schooling and education
- gatherings of friends and families

Each chapter in *Faithful Celebrations* begins with an Introduction that includes background material and key ideas for each celebration. Use this content to inspire your vision of what the event needs to be, for you, your planning committee, and your congregation or family. The pages that follow are organized by type of activity, such as opening prayer, story, craft, food, drama, music, game, or more. It will always conclude with a closing activity of prayer.

Each activity or experience will include a very brief explanation for the leader, followed by a list of materials needed and step-by-step directions. The materials called for in this book are simple and inexpensive. Those common to most activities are:

- Bibles
- whiteboard, poster board, or newsprint pad with markers
- felt pens
- crayons (regular and oversized for young children)
- drawing paper
- glue
- scissors

From time to time links will be offered to supplemental online materials; there are also downloadable resources of craft patterns and templates available for free at *www.churchpublishing.org/faithfulcelebrations4*.

> O God, you made us in your own image and redeemed us through Jesus your Son: Look with compassion on the whole human family; take away the arrogance and hatred which infect our hearts; break down the walls that separate us; unite us in bonds of love; and work through our struggle and confusion to accomplish your purposes on earth; that, in your good time, all nations and races may serve you in harmony around your heavenly throne; through Jesus Christ our Lord. *Amen.*
>
> —*For the Human Family*, Book of Common Prayer, p. 815

Chapter 1

NEW YEAR'S DAY

INTRODUCTION

> Therefore, since we are surrounded by so great a cloud of witnesses,
> let us also lay aside every weight and the sin that clings so closely,
> and let us run with perseverance the race that is set before us.
>
> —Hebrews 12:1–2

Reactions to the approach of a new year can vary wildly. Are you excited about the possibility of new beginnings and fresh starts? Do you already have your new exercise regimen outlined, the one you'll really stick with this time around? Are there house projects you plan to start (or finally complete)? Have you resolved to be kinder? more contemplative? undertake a new hobby?

Or are you simply trying to cope with the aftermath of Christmas, exhausted by the pressures of gift-giving, card-writing, party-attending, decorating, and putting up with cranky family members? Are you suffering from the post-holiday blues, the realization that Christmas never quite measures up to our culture's (and possibly your own) frenetic expectations?

Or perhaps you're among those that takes a "Bah, humbug!" approach to the entire notion of the start of a new year: "It's just another day, arbitrarily identified as the time to start anew. All our goodwill, cheer, and fresh starts are gone as soon as we get back to work, to school, to the same daily grind."

A BRIEF HISTORY OF NEW YEAR'S DAY

As long as there have been yearly calendars, there have been first days to each of those years, and it's part of human nature to look for these marked moments to view them as an opportunity to reflect and resolve. When did we begin to look at the start of each New Year on the calendar as a holiday?

We look to the Romans (who used the Julian calendar) to find the first "official" holiday linked to the start of the New Year. The Romans dedicated this day to Janus, appropriately the god of doorways and gates. From the name Janus comes our name for January—Janus was the god with two faces, who looked both backward and forward, in review of the year that had passed and in anticipation of the year starting.

Referring to Western culture, the Gregorian calendar, which became "official" in 1752, preserved January 1 as the start of the New Year. However, in different areas and at different times, other days were thought to start the New Year. For example, in England the Feast of the Annunciation, March 25, was regarded as the start of the New Year. The Chinese New Year falls between January 20 and February 20; the Hindu New Year normally falls on April 13 or 14; in Iran, it's the first day of spring; in Ethiopia, it's September 11 or 12. Yet around the world, January 1 is the most recognized start of the New Year, and probably the closest thing we have to a global holiday. Follow social media on December 31, and you'll see the New Year ushered in all day long as midnight arrives around the world.

New Year's Eve and New Year's Day celebrations vary from country to country, each with its own traditions. A great many of them, as in the United States, involve partying, fireworks, and waiting up until midnight to greet the new year. There are often parades on New Year's Day, as well as church services, family gatherings, local marathons for all ages, and, for some bizarre reason, plunges into ice-cold water (always optional).

For some liturgical churches, January 1 is also a holy day. For Catholics, it's the Solemnity of Mary, the Mother of God. Other churches observe January 1 as the Feast of the Circumcision of

Christ or Feast of the Holy Name; assuming Jesus was born on December 25, then, on the eighth day of his life, January 1, he would, according to Jewish tradition, have been circumcised and named in the Temple.

NEW YEAR'S DAY AND YOUR FAITH COMMUNITY

You may already have established traditions for how your church observes the arrival of the new year. You may have a New Year's Eve service and/or a New Year's morning service. You may provide a family-friendly New Year's Eve party. You could integrate many of these activities into a event you already have scheduled, but there's plenty here to plan your own unique and independent celebration of the new year, either on a weekend afternoon between Christmas and New Year's, on a weeknight, on New Year's Eve, or even on New Year's afternoon.

To get ready for a three-hour event resembling an actual "New Year's Eve" party, turn the clocks forward. For example, 6:00 p.m. becomes 9:00 p.m. and then the party will end at "midnight" for the kids. Whether you gather in your home, church, or community center, ring in the New Year with safe and fun experiences for all.

BEYOND THE CELEBRATION—SUPPORTING NEW YEAR'S RESOLUTIONS

Many people consider the start of a new year to be a time to give up old habits that they no longer want or feel aren't good for them and to begin a new habit, lifestyle, or rhythm. This often involves a feeling of wanting to take more responsibility for one's lifestyle or to get it back into a preferred lifestyle. The most common are losing weight or starting an exercise regime.

Being in a community such as the church is the perfect place to be supportive to people and families in these efforts. We all know that a resolution is much easier to keep if we have people to support us and hold us accountable. The church also teaches, throughout our scripture and liturgies, the process of repentance and *metanoia*—turning and changing our thoughts, habits, and orientation. These ideas are also important in the upcoming season of Lent.

What are the interests of your members and how might your church support and educate them? Is a weight loss program needed? How about starting an early morning or evening walking or running club? Perhaps what you need is a Wednesday evening supper with a homework room for kids and a short Bible study for adults? Are you in a community where many people need financial planning help or classes in parenting skills?

Ask and listen to what would be helpful in people's lives. And then offer some "New Year's Resolutions" classes in January.

- Do parents and children need homework help? Are there any retirees in your congregation who would give an hour a week to assist?

- Do people want to lose weight and exercise more? Can you start a weight loss program at your church? Perhaps there is someone already involved in one who will help you start a chapter at your church.

- Do people want a friend to walk with? Help people find each other; put up a bulletin board and include sign-up sheets organized by the major neighborhoods in your area. Include a line where people put down their address and phone numbers so that they can begin to organize themselves.

- Do parents of young children need a date night? Perhaps your youth groups would offer childcare to help raise funds for one of their mission trips. Or are there people who no longer have children in their home who would be willing to help with babysitting on a "date night"? This could be a church-wide event where you provide the childcare at your church.

WORSHIP

Opening Prayer

Begin with prayer and/or a litany to start your celebration:

> Come, Holy Spirit, Spirit of the Risen Christ, be with us today and always. Be our light, our guide, and our comforter. Be our strength, our courage, and our sanctifier. May this new year be a time of deep spiritual growth for us: a time of welcoming your graces and gifts, a time for forgiving freely and unconditionally, a time for growing in virtue and goodness. Come, Holy Spirit, be with us today and always. *Amen.*

Leader: The Lord God is awesome and worthy of praise.

Children: Let all that God has made rejoice.

All: Sun, moon, and morning stars; earth, seas, and all living creatures.

Leader: The glory of God is reflected in what God does.

Children: God invites all of us to be friends!

All: We are blessed because we worship the living God.

CELEBRATING OUR NAMES FEAST

Plan a worship event and meal to recognize the Feast of the Holy Name that is focused around a family-style meal. One candle in the center of each table would provide a focus for this service. Each family unit can provide a portion of the meal, which would need to be assigned and planned for in advance. While everyone is eating, offer conversation starters. Noted below, these can be written on signs for each table (placing them in inexpensive acrylic frames can make them noticeable for all to see).

Advance preparation

- Based on the estimated number of participants, invite each family, individual, or couple to bring a dish to share.

- Solicit help to set the tables before participants arrive.
- Print up conversation starters (one per table) and place them in acrylic frames or in another way to make them "stand out" on the tables.

Materials

- tables set for a family-style meal
- candles, holders, and matches
- food planned and assigned in advance
- *optional*: books of names and their meanings

Opening Prayer: "A Collect for The Holy Name," the Book of Common Prayer, p. 213

Eternal Father, you gave to your incarnate Son the holy name of Jesus to be the sign of our salvation: Plant in every heart, we pray, the love of him who is the Savior of the world, our Lord Jesus Christ; who lives and reigns with you and the Holy Spirit, one God, in glory everlasting. *Amen.*

Reading: Luke 2:15–21

When the angels had left them and gone into heaven, the shepherds said to one another, "Let us go now to Bethlehem and see this thing that has taken place, which the Lord has made known to us." So they went with haste and found Mary and Joseph, and the child lying in the manger. When they saw this, they made known what had been told them about this child; and all who heard it were amazed at what the shepherds told them. But Mary treasured all these words and pondered them in her heart. The shepherds returned, glorifying and praising God for all they had heard and seen, as it had been told them. After eight days had passed, it was time to circumcise the child; and he was called Jesus, the name given by the angel before he was conceived in the womb.

Prayer

God our Father, your son Jesus was born as a baby just as we were, and received the name of Jesus to be the Savior and Light of the world. In our baptism, we have been "marked as Christ's own forever," and named as your children. Give us such a deep love of Jesus that we may be a light in the world today in his name. This we ask through your Son, our Savior Jesus Christ, who lives with you and the Holy Spirit, now and forever. *Amen.*

Prayers

Invite individuals to pray for the world and others. Invite thanksgivings, particularly for blessings throughout the past year and for those who have died in the past year.

Meal Blessing

For these and all God's mercies, may God's holy Name be blessed and praised; through Jesus Christ Our Lord. *Amen.*

Conversation Starters

As noted above, these questions can be offered for discussion among members seated at the table during the meal. They can be written on tabletop signs or index cards placed on each table:

- What does it mean to be named?
- What is your full name? What do you know about it? For example, are you named for someone in your family, or do you know what your name means? (You could have a book of baby names and meanings available for people to look up their name.)
- What does our name say about us, individually and communally?
- Do you know what the name Jesus means? (Savior)
- Who gave Jesus his name? (See Luke 1:26–33.) Who gave you your name?

- When we are born and named, we become part of a family. This is also true when we are baptized—we are named, baptized with water in the "name of the Father, the Son, and the Holy Spirit" and then "marked as Christ's own forever." We become part of the family called the Church. We are now part of God's people. What does it mean to you to be part of the Church, part of God's people?

Conclusion of the Meal

The Lord bless you and keep you; the Lord make his face to shine upon you, and be gracious to you; the Lord lift up his countenance upon you, and give you peace.

—Numbers 6:24–25

CRAFTS

New Year's Hats

In one area of the celebration space, perhaps close to the entrance so that people are engaged as they arrive, create a craft center where people can choose a festive party hat and then embellish and customize it with various craft items. Encourage participants of every age to make a hat, supporting younger children with help as needed.

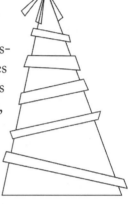

Be sure to cover the work area with news-print or craft paper and have cleaning supplies on hand to contain messes. Invite participants to wear their hats throughout the celebration, display their hats as a group as part of the celebration decorations, or use their hats as table décor or centerpieces.

Materials

- foam or paper party hats in various shapes and sizes (available from arts and crafts stores)
- various decorations: feathers, sequins, glitter glue, puff paint, stickers, washable markers
- washable glue

Confetti-Colored Noisemakers

Be prepared to make some noise once midnight strikes to wake up the new year.

Materials

- empty plastic water bottles with their caps, at least one per person (You can ask people to bring these with them or save them over a few weeks prior to your celebration.)
- dried beans

- 1 sheet white tissue paper per bottle
- scraps of tissue paper in various colors, cut into small shapes
- 24" long strips of any color of crepe paper streamer or ribbon (enough for several per bottle)
- white craft glue
- water
- scissors

Directions

1. Place a handful of beads inside a clean, dry water bottle. Run some glue around the mouth of the bottle and replace the cap.
2. Make a mixture of equal parts white craft glue and water.
3. Tear the white tissue paper into large strips or chunks, approximately 4" x 2".
4. All around the outside of the water bottle, paint the glue mixture onto a small section, apply the tissue paper, and add a second coat of the glue mixture on top of the paper. Repeat this process, covering the entire bottle with 2–3 coats of white tissue paper.
5. Apply small colorful squares of tissue paper randomly over the white tissue paper to resemble confetti.
6. If using the crepe paper streamers, cut each strip in half. Carefully tie one of the pieces around the neck of the bottle. Repeat with other lengths of crepe paper. Use scissors to cut each length to about 4" hanging length, and then cut upwards into thin strips. Use a couple pieces of the excess crepe paper you just cut off to twist around the neck of the bottle and glue in place. Allow to dry for several hours. If using the ribbons, tie around the neck of the bottle in lengths and colors as desired.
7. Shake and make some noise!

Spin-a-Drum Noisemaker

This homemade noisemaker is a hand drum based on a traditional Asian design.

Materials

- serrated knife (for adult-only use)
- empty oatmeal canister
- acrylic paint
- tacky glue
- glitter (optional)
- hole punch
- ½"-wide dowel, 1 foot long
- 16" length of string
- tape
- two ¾" wooden beads
- 2 plastic lids that fit the oatmeal canister
- paper
- ribbons

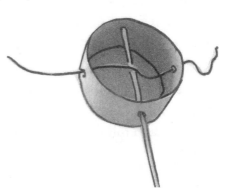

Directions

1. Have an adult use a serrated knife as a saw to cut a 1¾" ring from the top of the oatmeal canister. Neaten the cut edge with scissors.
2. Paint the outside of the ring, then add glue and glitter if desired. Let the paint and glue dry.
3. Punch a hole in the center of the ring's width. Punch additional, overlapping holes to gradually widen the hole just enough to fit the dowel.
4. Slide in the dowel so that it touches the inside of the ring. Secure the dowel to the ring with glue.
5. Punch two side holes in the ring directly opposite each other.

6. Wrap the ends of the string with small pieces of tape to make them easier to thread. Tie the center of the string to the dowel inside the ring.

7. Thread the ends through the holes and thread a bead on each end. Measure the string against the ring so that the beads will hit the center of the drumhead. Knot the end of the string and snip off the excess.

8. Place the two plastic lids onto the sides of the ring.

9. Cut paper circles to fit the tops of the lids, decorate them, and glue them in place.

10. Tie ribbons to the dowel at the drum's base.

11. Play the drum by holding the dowel upright between your palms and rolling it quickly back and forth so that the beads hit the lids.

A Year of Time

> For everything there is a season, and a time for every matter under heaven: a time to be born, and a time to die; a time to plant, and a time to pluck up what is planted; a time to kill, and a time to heal; a time to break down, and a time to build up; a time to weep, and a time to laugh; a time to mourn, and a time to dance; a time to throw away stones, and a time to gather stones together; a time to embrace, and a time to refrain from embracing; a time to seek, and a time to lose; a time to keep, and a time to throw away; a time to tear, and a time to sew; a time to keep silence, and a time to speak; a time to love, and a time to hate; a time for war, and a time for peace.
>
> —Ecclesiastes 3:1–8

The times of our lives—birthdays, anniversaries, holidays, seasons—give our life a rhythm. They help us to mark time. New Year's Eve and New Year's Day are two of these markers of time—they mark the end of the old year and the beginning of the new. It's an end and a beginning. This rhythm or marking of time also serves to locate us in time. It teaches us about the created world and how it is ordered and works. It teaches us how our families work and celebrate major occasions and events. As we look into the year to come, we also take a look back at the previous year. We see twelve months, fifty-two weeks, 365 days, 8,760 hours, 525,600 minutes, 31,536,000 seconds. And all is a gift from God. We have done nothing to deserve it, earn it, or purchase it. Like the air we breathe, time comes to us as a part of life.

The gift of time is not ours alone. It is given equally to each person. Rich and poor, educated and ignorant, strong and weak—every man, woman, and child has the same twenty-four hours every day. And we cannot stop time. There is no way to slow it down, turn it off, or adjust it. Time marches on.

You also can't bring back time. Once it is gone, it is gone. Yesterday is lost forever. If yesterday is lost, tomorrow is uncertain. Obviously, time is one of our most precious possessions. We can waste it. We can worry over it. We can spend it on ourselves. Or, as good stewards, we can invest it in the kingdom of God.

The new year is full of time. As a community, reflect on the past year through words and pictures.

Materials

- 8' strip of butcher paper or newsprint
- masking tape
- markers and crayons

Directions

1. Tape the piece of butcher paper along a wall. Make sure paper is hung at an accessible height for all participants. If using newsprint squares, tape them together end-to-end.
2. Make a horizontal line across the center of the paper.
3. Mark off the twelve months of the previous year in even segments.
4. Provide markers and crayons and invite people to write down significant events of the past year. Young and old alike may

choose to draw pictures as their contribution. These events can focus on events in people's lives (children will love to add their birthdays); events in the world, nation, and your community; or events in your family or congregation.

5. As a group, invite participants to walk the length of the timeline, explaining to the group what they see and what they have added along the way. How can the New Year be filled with time well used?

Thank-You Notes

While we are still in the season of Christmas, it is time to reflect and give thanks for all that we received during the past few days—including all those presents. In his Letter to the Galatians, Paul reminds us of the most wonderful privilege in the world we have been given—being chosen as God's own adopted daughters and sons.

Materials

- construction paper or white paper
- pens, pencils, crayons, markers
- envelopes
- stamps

Directions

1. Distribute materials and invite individuals to write a thank-you note to God, telling God how grateful they are to be God's own adopted child and how they will try to live as a faithful son or daughter of God.

2. Optionally, invite everyone to then write thank-you notes to all those who gave them presents for Christmas.

3. Adults or youth can help non-writers with this task . . . or encourage simple drawings instead of words.

4. If it seems appropriate, at some point in the celebration, invite volunteers (do not force sharing) to share their letters to God.

5. Provide envelopes to take home (and mail to the recipient if applicable) after the celebration, keeping the one to God handy as a reminder throughout the coming year.

Wax Castings

Every year is a new beginning, a "pure" time of a new creation. The uproar and noise-making that still is a part of our modern New Year's celebration is an ancient expression of blasting away the devils and evil spirits, the faults and failings that represent "old time," and a purging and purification that allows a renewal and regeneration of creation.

Invite participants to bring old candle stubs to your gathering. Perhaps these represent events that have occurred during the past year: birthday celebrations, special occasions, family dinners, etc. With what has been old and used, make something new and creative.

Materials

- short, used candle stubs
- empty coffee cans (or large tin cans)
- large pot filled with hot water
- ladle
- large pot filled with ice and ice water

Directions (make sure adults are helping children)

1. Each individual or family melts down their candle stubs in an old coffee can set in a hot water bath.
2. Once melted, each person pours a ladle of hot wax into a pot of ice and ice water.
3. The casting that results is a fantastic shape and the inspiration for the "reading" of the individual's past year and future possibilities.
4. Each person can take a turn being the "seer," "reading" another person's new wax casting.

Kakizome

On January 2, there is a Japanese tradition called *kakizome*—the first writings of the year. The custom started long ago when people wrote haiku and other poems of happiness to start the new year. Today people write poems or proverbs on long strips of paper in beautiful calligraphy and hang them for all to admire.

Materials

- white strips of paper 4¼" x 11"
- black ink or tempera paint
- ½" paint brushes
- newspaper
- scrap paper
- pencils
- Bibles

Directions

1. Using scrap paper, write a poem (haiku or other) or a favorite proverb (look them up in the Bible).
2. Cover a table with newsprint.
3. With the white paper lengthwise on the table, pencil the poem or proverb.
4. Painting with even brush strokes, trace over the words so that it looks like calligraphy.
5. Hang to dry—and for all to see.

More on Haiku

In Japanese tradition, these finished resolutions are hung and celebrated. To quote one Japanese proverb, "The very thing one likes, one does well."

Haiku is a poetic form and a type of poetry from the Japanese culture. Haiku combines form, content, and language in a meaningful, yet compact form. Haiku poets write about everyday things.

Many themes include nature, feelings, or experiences. Usually they use simple words and grammar. The most common form for Haiku is three short lines:

- The first line usually contains five syllables.
- The second line contains seven syllables.
- The third and final line contains five syllables.

Haiku doesn't rhyme. A Haiku must "paint" a mental image in the reader's mind. This is the challenge of Haiku—to put the poem's meaning and imagery in the reader's mind in only seventeen syllables over just three lines of poetry.

STORYTELLING AND BIBLE STUDY

Reflecting on the Gift of Life

In the gospel reading for the Holy Name of Our Lord, Luke tells us that Mary treasured in her heart—and reflected on—all the mysterious happenings that surrounded Jesus' birth.

Materials

- Gift of Life Questionnaire (see below or download at *www. churchpublishing.org/faithfulcelebrations4*)

Directions

1. Read Luke 2:15–21 (found on page 6) aloud.
2. Encourage participants of all ages to talk with others about the days of their own births or adoptions.
3. Children can talk with a parent about the day of their birth or adoption and the circumstances that surrounded it.
4. Name some of the important things you want to remember about the day of your birth or have parents share this information with their children.

Information to learn about or share

My name _____

My date of birth _____

The time I was born _____

How much I weighed _____

The date of my baptism _____

Some things family and friends said about me_____

Feast of the Holy Name Bible Study

The readings assigned for January 1 (the Holy Name) support the theme of incorporation into the people of God. The Old Testament passage is one of blessing that sets the tone for this Feast of the Holy Name. The Gospel tells us of that event in connection with the bestowing of the name of Jesus—so that all generations would bless his Holy Name.

The naming of Mary's child was a part of the great unfolding of God's plan for salvation of the world. By the directive of an angel, her Child was given the name that means Yahweh saves— so that he would grow up to fulfill his vocation as Savior of the world. In biblical tradition, every male child was formally named and circumcised on the eighth day after birth. In many societies circumcision is observed as a rite of passage. In Judaism—where ritual circumcision is known as *berith* or bris—it is said to be the sign of the covenant established between God and Abraham: "This is my covenant, which you shall keep, between me and you and your offspring after you: Every male among you shall be circumcised" (Genesis 17:10).

Lead group members in the following discussion:

- Reflect on the importance of names and naming. What is our response to the Holy Names of God and Jesus?
- What is revealed about the nature of God and God's relation to humanity?
- Reflect on your own name. What does it mean for you? If you were to change your name, what name would you choose, and why?

Continue by reading and discussing one or more of the following scriptures:

Psalm 8

- What do the words of the psalmist tell us about God, as well as about our own humanity?
- What is our responsibility to God and to God's creation?

Galatians 4:4–7 or Philippians 2:5–11

- In Galatians we read that Jesus came for our redemption, and so that we might become heirs of God. What does it mean that we are adopted as God's children?
- Does it really matter that we know the name of Jesus?

Luke 2:15–21

- We read that the shepherds left their fields to "see this thing that has taken place." What might they have been thinking as they approached Bethlehem? What do you think they expected to find?
- Verse 18 tells us that as the shepherds shared their experience with others, "all who heard it were amazed." As we read the familiar words of the Nativity narrative, how does this story continue to be amazing to us today?
- In a sense, the shepherds were the first evangelists. During this Christmas season, as well as throughout the year, what can we do to proclaim the birth of the Messiah?
- Imagine the scene that is described in the gospel passage. What do you think Mary pondered in her heart?
- Imagine you are the parent of the infant Jesus. How do you think you would respond to the events described here?
- How does Jesus' name speak to us of his life and ministry, his salvation for us?

MUSIC

The Twelve Days of Need

The song "The Twelve Days of Christmas" is an English or French Christmas carol dating to the eighteenth century. In this cumulative song (where each verse builds on the previous one), the gifts get grander each day. The song is fun to sing because of its cumulative nature and the fun that can be added to trying to remember all the gifts. It can also remind us that Christmas is not just a day, but also a season in the Christian calendar.

In most of the Western Church, Christmas season begins on December 25 and lasts until January 5, Epiphany Eve. Epiphany celebrates the coming of the Magi with their gifts for the Christ Child. In many cultures, Christmas season, these twelve days of Christmas, are also a time for gift-giving, whether it be a small present each day, or a special recognition or thanksgiving for someone else.

Directions

1. With group members, sing (or at least review) the words to "The Twelve Days of Christmas."

2. Invite the group to come up with its own version of the song, rewriting the words to:

   - reflect gifts for which people would be thankful today
   - reflect gifts for which your family or congregation is thankful

3. Publicize this "Twelve Top Needs" for donations of time, money, service, supplies, etc.

4. Share the song with others at this gathering celebration or in the context of Sunday worship in one or more ways, such as:

   - Make a plan to either perform the song or publicize it in the church bulletin.
   - Make posters for the church entryway or church hall.
   - Assign each line item to someone or some group.

"Auld Lang Syne" Group Sing

"Auld Lang Syne" is a Scots poem written by Robert Burns in 1788 and set to the tune of a traditional folk song. The song's Scots title may be translated into English literally as "old long since," or more idiomatically, "long, long ago," "days gone by," or "old times." Consequently "For auld lang syne," as it appears in the first line of the chorus, is loosely translated as "for (the sake of) old times."

Traditionally sung at the conclusion of a New Year gathering in Scotland and around the world, it is common practice that everyone joins hands with the person next to them to form a great circle around the dance floor. At the beginning of the last verse, everyone crosses their arms across their breast, so that the right hand reaches out to the neighbor on the left and vice versa. When the tune ends, everyone rushes to the middle, while still holding hands. When the circle is re-established, everyone turns under the arms to end up facing outwards with hands still joined.

Advance preparation

- While most people know the first verse and chorus of the song, few will know all the verses. Consider copying the words to whiteboard, poster board, or flip chart.

Materials

- whiteboard, flip chart, or poster board
- markers

Directions

1. Share some (or all) of the background information on the song offered above.
2. Take some time teaching the song to those who might be unfamiliar with it. Younger children can join in chorus, even if they can't read all the words.
3. Consider singing the song with the motions described above.

Auld Lang Syne (in English)

Should old acquaintance be forgot,
and never brought to mind?
Should old acquaintance be forgot,
and auld lang syne?

Chorus:

For auld lang syne, my dear,
for auld lang syne,
we'll take a cup of kindness yet,
for auld lang syne.

And surely you'll buy your pint cup!
and surely I'll buy mine!
And we'll take a cup o' kindness yet,
for auld lang syne.

Chorus

We two have run about the slopes,
and picked the daisies fine;
But we've wandered many a weary foot,
since auld lang syne.

Chorus

We two have paddled in the stream,
from morning sun till dine;
But seas between us broad have roared
since auld lang syne.

Chorus

And there's a hand my trusty friend!
And give us a hand o' thine!
And we'll take a right good-will draught,
for auld lang syne.

Chorus

GAMES

Flashlight Limbo

In this lights-out version of a classic party game, the object is to avoid the beam of the flashlight.

Materials

- two flashlights
- music from a digital device or CD player

Directions

1. Clear a floor space and turn off the lights.
2. Two people, each holding a flashlight, stand a few feet apart, turn on the flashlights, and point them at each other to create a level beam of light for the others to limbo under.
3. Play seasonal music to liven things up.

Charades

Ring in the new year with this silly game in which players act out notable events of the past twelve months.

Materials

- paper
- pens or markers
- two baskets or hats
- watch or timer

Directions

1. Divide the players into two teams and send the teams into separate rooms. Each group should then write an agreed-upon number of events from the past year on slips of paper. (Try to list only events that most players will be likely to remember

such as an event everyone attended, a favorite movie that debuted, or a significant local news event.)

2. Fold the slips in half, then collect each team's slips in a separate basket or hat and have the teams return to the playing area.

3. To play, determine a time limit for each performance, then have players take turns pulling slips from the other team's container and pantomiming the event mentioned, offering clues (such as the type of event, the number of words, and so on) as in regular charades, if you like.

4. If any of the actor's teammates can correctly identify the incident before time runs out, that team earns one point.

5. The highest score team after all the events have been acted out wins.

PRAYER ACTIVITY

Out with the Old—Bring in the New

Fire holds a fascination for children and adults alike and is a powerful symbol of change and transformation. In cultures from Scotland to the Congo, blazing bonfires are a big part of New Year's Eve. This simple activity (performed, of course, with adult supervision) is one way of bringing that ancient enchantment home.

Materials

- lightweight white paper (such as onionskin or tracing paper)
- pencils or pens
- fireplace, fire pit, or small grill, like a hibachi (or metal bowl or pan)
- candle and candlestick
- envelopes

Directions

1. Invite each participant to write down on a small slip of lightweight paper something from the last year that he or she would like to get rid of—an unwanted habit or something one wishes to put in the past, like a bad experience or wrongdoing.

2. One by one, each participant steps forward and hands the paper to a designated adult, who lights it with a candle and carefully places it in the fireplace or container to burn and disappear.

3. Part two of the ceremony is equally important: Everyone writes down his or her wishes for the future and places them in a sealed envelope that is kept in a safe spot for a year—to be opened and re-read next New Year's Eve, when the cycle begins again.

FAITH IN ACTION

Outreach in the New Year

> For I was hungry and you gave me food, I was thirsty and you gave me something to drink, I was a stranger and you welcomed me.
>
> —Matthew 25:35

The first day of a new year is a great time to look ahead with confidence and joy. Maybe this year will be the year your sports team will win, that you'll meet the right person or get the right job, that everyone's dreams will come true. And who's to say that's not possible?

Also, maybe this is the year we do something effective about hunger. The world focuses on times of feast or famine, but our Christian belief makes us more rooted than that. We can learn more about the work that Christian agencies do to advocate for hunger around the globe. Research the various agencies and choose a project to be involved in as a family or church community in the coming year through letter writing, donations, and awareness:

- Bread for the World—*www.bread.org*
- Garden Harvest—*www.facebook.com/pg/gardenharvest*
- CROP and Church World Service—*www.churchworldservice.org*
- Episcopal Relief and Development—*www.er-d.org*
- The Presbyterian Hunger Program—*www.pcusa.org/hunger*
- ELCA World Hunger—*www.elca.org/Our-Work/Relief -and-Development/ELCA-World-Hunger*
- United Methodist Committee on Relief—*www.umcor.org*

RECIPES

How communities and families celebrate New Year's Day is unique to them. One visible way that we can see this difference is through food. In your community (and/or region of the United States or Canada), is there such a custom around food? This custom could also revolve around different ethnic groups.

Invite your planning committee or another group to discuss and investigate this:

- If there are food customs associated with New Year's Day, what are they?
- Do some families in your church have certain customs around New Year's Day, and would they be willing to share that with others?
- How can you incorporate these into your celebration?

If there is not such a custom, adopt one from another part of the country or a specific ethnic group and make it the theme of your event. For example, in the southern United States, custom or folklore teaches people that for good luck in the new year you have to eat these foods on New Year's Day:

- pork
- stewed tomatoes
- collard greens
- black-eyed peas (or Hoppin' John)
- cornbread

Hoppin' John Parfait (Serves 6 to 8)

Ingredients

- 2 bacon strips, cut into 1" pieces
- 2 cups chopped red or green bell pepper

- ¼ cup diced onion
- 1 tomato, chopped
- ¼ teaspoon chili powder
- salt and pepper to taste
- 2 cups fresh or frozen black-eyed peas
- 3 cups chicken broth
- 2 cups cooked rice
- 1 cup grated Cheddar cheese
- sour cream and cherry tomatoes (for garnish)

Directions

1. In a medium saucepan, sauté the bacon for five minutes.
2. Stir in ½ cup of the bell pepper, the onion, the chopped tomato, the chili powder, the salt and pepper, and the black-eyed peas.
3. Pour in the broth and bring the mixture to a low boil, then simmer it uncovered for 1 hour or more, stirring occasionally, until the liquid is absorbed.
4. Layer the peas, rice, cheese, and remaining bell pepper in parfait glasses.
5. Top with sour cream and a cherry tomato.

Godcake Muffins

On New Year's Day in many cultures, parents and grandparents are specially honored. A British custom from Coventry, England, is that a child and its godparents visit on this day; the godparents offer the child a blessing and a "godcake," which is a sweet pastry shaped like a triangle. An afternoon of visiting, tea, and/or supper is followed by evening prayer.

Inspired by this practice, celebrate a contemporary version of this custom with those who are assembled. Make some muffins and gather with candles for prayer and song.

Ingredients

- ½ cup raisins
- 2 cups flour
- 1 cup sugar
- 2 teaspoons baking soda
- 2 teaspoons cinnamon
- ½ teaspoon ground ginger
- ½ teaspoon salt
- 2 cups peeled, grated carrot
- 1 large tart apple, grated
- ½ cup sweetened shredded coconut, not the moist kind
- ½ cup sliced almonds or chopped walnuts
- ⅓ cup sunflower seeds or wheat germ
- 3 large eggs
- ⅔ cup vegetable oil
- 2 teaspoons vanilla extract

Supplies

- muffin tins
- grease for muffin tins, or paper baking cups
- oven
- hot pads or potholders

Directions

1. Preheat oven to 375°F.
2. Grease muffin tins (or line with papers).
3. Cover raisins with hot water and set aside.
4. Mix eggs, oil, and vanilla; set aside.
5. Mix flour, sugar, baking soda, spices, and salt.

6. Add remaining ingredients (carrots, apple, coconut, nuts, sunflower seeds or wheat germ). Mix well.

7. Add egg/oil mixture and stir until combined.

8. Add drained raisins and mix.

9. Pour batter into muffin tins.

10. Bake for 20–25 minutes.

Note: This recipe makes 12 large or 15 medium muffins.

WORSHIP

Closing Prayers

Conclude by praying either or both of these closing prayers, or another prayer of your own choosing. An option could be to distribute sparklers at the end of your celebration, too.

> May God keep us from all harm and bless us with every
>   good gift.
> May God's Word be in our hearts and give us joy.
> May we walk in God's ways and know God's peace. *Amen.*

> Creator God, you blessed us with earth's abundance, and charged us with stewardship for your creation. Your prophets called us to faithfulness, to bring good news to the poor and to proclaim Jubilee. Bless these letters and with them our gifts of faith and citizenship. May your message ring out through our words and deeds. Open the eyes and hearts of our leaders, that we may as a nation rise to the challenge and dedicate our resources to ending hunger in your world. Thus may we see the light of Christ shine forth to all the ends of the earth. *Amen.*
>
> —from the Christian Reformed Church

> Most gracious and merciful God, you have reconciled us to yourself through Jesus Christ your Son, and called us to new life in him: Grant that we, who begin this year in his Name, may complete it to his honor and glory; who lives and reigns now and forever. *Amen.*
>
> —from *The Book of Occasional Services*[1]

---

1. *The Book of Occasional Services* (New York: Church Publishing, 2004), 45.

Chapter 2

MARTIN LUTHER KING JR. DAY

INTRODUCTION

Martin Luther King Jr. was the preeminent leader in the Civil Rights Movement in the United States. As Christians we are called to strive for justice and peace and to respect the dignity of every person.

The Federal holiday set aside to honor the life of Dr. Martin Luther King Jr. is the only such holiday created to honor a single individual. It's a fitting tribute to the man whom many consider the most prominent civil rights leader of the twentieth century. Schools are closed and many municipalities offer services and observances, with all ages gathered to learn about the ministry of Dr. King and perform a "day of service" in his name in the community.

King was born in 1929 into a family with a rich tradition of Baptist clergymen, including his father and grandfather. Following in their footsteps he attended Morehouse College, an institution noted for the education of black Americans. After receiving a doctorate from Boston University, he became pastor of Dexter Avenue Baptist Church in Montgomery, Alabama.

His Christian faith led him to the cause of civil rights in the segregated South of post-World War II America. He travelled to India and was greatly inspired by studying Gandhi's philosophy of nonviolent protest. His leadership helped win a great victory for the Bus Boycott of 1956, which ended in the desegregation of the buses. In 1957 he became president of the Southern Christian Leadership Conference and helped synthesize a strategy combining the Christian ideals of peace and justice with Gandhi's strategy of nonviolent protest.

During the following eleven years, King became the unquestioned leader for the Civil Rights Movement in the United States, travelling millions of miles and giving thousands of speeches. His famous "I Have a Dream" speech in Washington was attended by a quarter of a million people. He was frequently arrested and was personally assaulted several times, but he saw his efforts rewarded in 1964 with the passage of the Civil Rights Act and in 1965 with the passage of the Voting Rights Act.

As his worldwide stature grew, King became an icon not only for black people in America, but for people everywhere who suffered injustice and oppression. In 1964 at the age of thirty-five he became the youngest person to ever receive the Nobel Peace Prize, and his acceptance speech is still read and studied throughout the world.

Dr. King was assassinated on April 4, 1968 in Memphis, Tennessee, where he had gone to lead a rally in support of striking street cleaners. He is remembered on that day on the calendar of the Episcopal Church for his outstanding witness to the dignity of every human being and his life's work for peace and justice.

Suggestions for Leaders

- Read over the directions for each study, movie, or activity. Check your licensing agreement to be sure that you can legally show a movie. Gather all supplies in one place. Do any activity prep before the celebration begins. A list of supplies is given for each activity.

- Don't forget to answer these questions in your planning:

    ◦ Who is our audience for this celebration—our own congregation and/or the wider community?

- ○ *Where* will we hold the event, indoors or out? What is "Plan B" if it rains?
- ○ *When* will the celebration take place? What is the schedule?
- ○ What supplies will we need? (*Be very specific.*)
- ○ *Who* will be responsible for what aspects of the celebration?

- At every Baptism we attend in the Episcopal Church there is a series of five promises that we affirm during the liturgy of Holy Baptism. The fourth promise is, "Will you seek and serve Christ in all persons, loving your neighbor as yourself?" The last promise is, "Will you strive for justice and peace among all people, and respect the dignity of every human being?" And we reply to both, "I will, with God's help." As you prepare for this celebration, consider:

  - ○ How do you think what we are celebrating helps us live into these promises?
  - ○ What can *you* do to live into these promises? to help others live into these promises?

Beyond the Celebration

- Encourage participants to make their own prayer center at home. They can use a colored placemat or piece of colored construction paper. They can place their Bible on this mat along with sacred objects that remind them of Martin Luther King Jr. Sacred objects can be anything that has special meaning for you in your faith. A candle and a picture of Jesus or a cross could be included. Place this on a table where you eat meals or in some central place where the family gathers.
- In the sacrament of Baptism we are made a member of God's family. In a way we are adopted and given a new name—"Christian"—as we are marked and sealed as Christ's own forever. In this larger "family" we have opportunities and privileges to honor those who have respected the dignity of every person and who continue to strive for justice and peace.

At home around the dinner table, in other groups you may already attend, or perhaps in a forum like an online blog or on your church's website, continue to explore what it means to work for justice and peace.

- Invite speakers from the Union of Black Episcopalians (*www.ube.org*) to come speak to a gathering or to deliver the sermon/homily at a church service.

- Partner with other faith communities to hold a joint service filled with song and speakers to commemorate Dr. King's life and legacy, as well as to advocate for continuing justice.

WORSHIP

Begin your celebration with this prayer by Marie Fowler found in *Race and Prayer: Collected Voices, Many Dreams*[1]:

> On this day when we honor the life of Martin Luther King Jr.
>   and his courage and vision,
> Grant us the grace to dream of a society, a world, where our
>   differences will not divide us,
> But rather enable us.
> Grant us the humility to learn from each other, to try new
>   ways, explore new paths.
> That we can turn and see that children everywhere are children
> Regardless of color or language, religion or custom.
> Perhaps it is too late for us, who remember the hurt of exclusion
>   and prejudice
> Who encounter it still.
> But, working together, we can dream of a better world where all
>   our children will be
> "Free at last! Free at last!" *Amen.*

Worship Center

Create a focal point for your celebration to keep the image and memory of Martin Luther King Jr. present during your event.

Materials

- candle and matches
- icon (picture or symbol for Christ)
- icon of Martin Luther King Jr. (or some symbol of his ministry)
- green placemat or cloth
- Bible

---

1. Marie Fowler, *Race and Prayer: Collected Voices, Many Dreams*, edited by Malcolm Boyd and Chester Talton (New York: Morehouse, 2003).

Directions

On a small table in the center of the room or in the middle of the table (if all are sitting around one table), place a candle, an icon or symbol for Christ, and an icon of Martin Luther King Jr. (*www.trinitystores.com/artwork/martin-luther-king-georgia*) or some symbol of his ministry on a green placemat or cloth. Place a Bible on the table as well, open to the Exodus story (chapter 15). Light the candle.

Choose from this selection of prayers to use when appropriate throughout your celebration:

> Almighty God, by the hand of Moses your servant you led your people out of slavery, and made them free at last: Grant that your Church, following the example of your prophet Martin Luther King, may resist oppression in the name of your love, and may secure for all your children the blessed liberty of the Gospel of Jesus Christ; who lives and reigns with you and the Holy Spirit, one God, now and for ever. *Amen.*
>
> —Martin Luther King Jr., *Lesser Feasts and Fasts*, p. 217

> Grant, O God, that your holy and life-giving Spirit may so move every human heart and especially the hearts of the people of this land, that barriers which divide us may crumble, suspicions disappear, and hatreds cease; that our divisions being healed, we may live in justice and peace; through Jesus Christ our Lord. *Amen.*
>
> —Book of Common Prayer, p. 823

> Gracious, loving, and compassionate God of our fathers and mothers, we give you thanks for your faithful servants in every age who have struggled against injustice and oppression and who have fought to root out the evil and sin of racism and discrimination. Through witnesses such as Harriet Tubman, Absalom Jones, and Martin Luther King Jr., we have learned the merits of self-sacrifice, courageous action, and redemptive

suffering. Grant that we in this day, following their example, may continue to resist oppression in all its forms and guises. In this month of commemoration and celebration, may we resolve to remain committed to do the work to which you have called each of us and which you require of us all—"to do justly, love mercy, and walk humbly" with you, our God. Trusting in your grace and mercy and in the power of your holy enabling and sustaining Spirit, we ask this in the name of our Liberator, your Son Jesus Christ. *Amen.*

—"A Prayer for Black History Month"
by the Rt. Rev. Barbara C. Harris,
in *Race and Prayer: Collected Voices, Many Dreams*[2]

2. Fowler, *Race and Prayer*, 178.

CRAFTS

"Freedom Quilt" Squares

Read one of the books about freedom quilts listed below. The American folksong "Follow the Drinking Gourd," first published in 1928, is a folktale about an Underground Railroad operative who encoded escape instructions and a map. These directions then enabled fleeing slaves to make their way north from Mobile, Alabama, to the Ohio River and freedom. Metaphorically the "drinking gourd" refers to the hollowed out gourd used by slaves (and other rural Americans) as a water dipper. But here it is used as a code name for the Big Dipper star formation, which points to Polaris, the Pole Star, and north—toward freedom.

- *Follow the Drinking Gourd* by Jeanette Winter
- *I Lay My Stitches Down: Poems of American Slavery* by Cynthia Grady
- *Sweet Clara and the Freedom Quilt* by Deborah Hopkinson
- *Hidden in Plain View: A Secret Story of Quilts and the Underground Railroad* by Jacqueline L. Tobin and Raymond G. Dobard
- *The Patchwork Path: A Quilt Map to Freedom* by Bettye Stroud
- *The Quilts of Gee's Bend: Masterpieces from a Lost Place* by William Arnett, Alvia Wardlaw, Jane Livingston, and John Beardsley
- *Stitchin' and Pullin': A Gee's Bend Quilt* by Patricia McKissack and Cozbi A. Cabrera
- *Signs and Symbols: African Images in African-American Quilts* by Maude Southwell Wahlman

Following the sharing and discussion of the story, invite participants to construct a square for a quilt. If desired, all the squares can be assembled for one large "quilt," which can be put on display throughout the month of February.

Materials

- foam-core board cut in 6" x 6" squares (available at local craft and hobby stores)
- rolls of electrical tape in a variety of colors
- scissors
- *optional:* books of quilt patterns

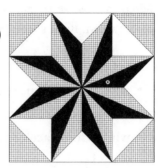

Directions

1. Cut one square of foam-core board 6" x 6" for each participant.
2. Choose a design from one of the pattern books or these quilting sites (or make up your own):
    - *https://www.owensoundtourism.ca/en/arts-and-culture/quilt-codes.aspx*
    - *http://pathways.thinkport.org/secrets/secret_quilt.cfm*
3. Use a variety of colored electrical tape to "piece together" your quilt.

Alternative directions

1. Cut your 6" x 6" quilt "squares," then punch holes all around the perimeter every 2–3 inches.
2. Place all the quilt squares in your desired pattern and then "sew" them together with the yarn.
3. Have each participant sign their quilt square on the backside.
4. If at some point you want to disassemble the quilt, simply cut the yarn.

Shekere Musical Instruments

The *shekere* is an instrument from West Africa consisting of a dried gourd with beads woven into a net covering the gourd. Throughout the continent there are similar gourd/bead or gourd/seed percussion instruments. Some are the *lilolo*, *axatse* (Ghana), *djabara* (Guinea), *ushàkà,* and *chequere.* It is predominantly called *shekere* in Nigeria. Make a *shekere* to accompany your music and singing during the celebration. Find some songs on pages 48–49.

Materials

- gourd, paper cup, or toilet paper tube (1 per participant)
- rice and/or dried beans
- white Con-Tact® paper
- waxed paper
- rubber bands
- CD player or digital device with lively music, preferably related to today's session, such as a collection of African-American spirituals

Directions

1. Fill a gourd, paper cup, or toilet paper tube with rice or dried beans and seal the top using Con-Tact® paper or waxed paper held in place with a rubber band.
2. Play the music (or sing the hymns) and invite everyone to play along with their instruments.
3. Invite everyone to dance along as well.

STORYTELLING AND BIBLE STUDY
Book Corner

Gather some of the books listed below from your local school or church library. Place pillows on the floor for children to sit or lay upon while reading. Most of the books listed are appropriate for children eight years old and older. Books that involve the folklore of quilts and slavery can be found on page 40 and can also be included in your book corner.

If you choose to read aloud one or more of the stories in a group, use the following questions to spur conversation:

- What did you learn from this book? Did you learn something new?
- How is the gospel message of love represented in the main character?
- What could you do differently because you read this book?
- Does this book remind you of other stories?

Possible titles

- *Moses: When Harriet Tubman Led Her People to Freedom* by Carole Boston Weatherford
- *The Beatitudes: From Slavery to Civil Rights* by Carole Boston Weatherford
- *Let My People Go* by Patricia and Fredrick McKissack
- *If You Lived at the Time of Martin Luther King* by Ellen Levine
- *Martin's Big Words: The Life of Dr. Martin Luther King Jr.* by Doreen and Bryan Collier Rapport
- *DK Biography: Martin Luther King Jr.* by Amy Pastan and Primo Levi
- *Strength to Love* by Martin Luther King Jr.
- *If A Bus Could Talk: The Story of Rosa Parks* by Faith Ringgold
- *Rosa Parks: A Life* by Douglas G. Brinkley
- *Amazing Grace: William Wilberforce and the Heroic Campaign to End Slavery* by Eric Metaxas
- *The Story of Ruby Bridges* by Robert Coles

"Lamentations and Joy" Bible Study

Choose from the following scriptures, as appropriate for your group. Some stories will be appropriate for all ages; some may be challenging even for older participants. You could also consider reading a chosen story to the youngest participants from a children's Bible, including one with illustrations.

- Exodus 14–15
- Psalms 126, 77, or 98:1–4
- Isaiah 42:5–9
- Isaiah 61:1–4
- Ecclesiastes 4:1–3
- Micah 6:8
- Amos 5:23–24
- Matthew 5:3–12
- Luke 6:27–36
- Luke 10:25–37
- John 15:12–15

Materials

- Bibles
- pens or pencils
- paper

Directions

1. Provide Bibles, pencils, and paper for participants.
2. Divide into smaller groups of 4–6 people each.
3. Ask for three volunteers *within each small group* to read the chosen scripture passage or story, using this method:

   - Read the passage the first time.
   - Discuss briefly what the passage tells us about God.
   - Read the passage a second time.
   - Discuss what the passage tells us about human beings (men, women, and children; young and old; different races; and different places) and the relationship between people.
   - Read the passage a third time.
   - Discuss what the passage tells us about the relationship between God and human beings. How might people living

in different circumstances or in different cultures perceive the passage's message about the relationship between God and human beings? How does the passage call us (individually and corporately) to change?

4. Regather as a large group and invite a volunteer representative from each group to succinctly share their group's discussion.

5. Read the passage aloud, quietly—meditatively—as a closing prayer. Leave a moment of silence.

6. Discuss together:

   • Where do you find yourself in the Bible passage?
   • Where do you find this celebration's theme in the Bible passage?

The Call to Justice

Since Dr. King's assassination in 1968, his birthday on January 15 has been honored with speeches, sharing Dr. King's values of the American Dream, equal opportunity, and that one day white and black children might be judged by "the content of their character . . . [and not] by the color of their skin." How do we do justice to Dr. King's commitment to social justice that involves (as it did for him) personal faith, the New Testament's gospel of unconditional love, and the Old Testament's prophetic insistence on righteous justice. "It is not enough for us to talk about love," he told his followers. "There is another side called justice. . . . Standing beside love is always justice. Not only are we using the tools of persuasion—we've got to use the tools of coercion."

The Bible contains many call stories, stories of ordinary people called to serve the purpose of God, including Moses, Samuel, David, Mary, and the disciples. For whatever reason, God chooses to further the Kingdom of Heaven through the lives of ordinary people—people called far beyond what they believed possible—Harriet Tubman, Absalom Jones, Richard Allen, Sojourner Truth, William Wilberforce, Abraham Lincoln, Martin Luther King,

Marian Anderson, Rosa Parks, the Tuskegee Airmen, the Buffalo Soldiers, and countless unnamed people who went far beyond what they believed possible.

This Bible study incorporates the stories of the prophets and others who were called by God to challenge the world around them. In addition, bring "modern" voices (see pages 52–57) to your study by reading and discussing (or children may wish to illustrate) their words of justice for the world.

Materials

- Bibles
- Biographic information found on pages 52–57

Directions

1. Distribute Bibles and/or the biographic information about more contemporary individuals.
2. In small groups, or individually, read aloud each "person's" call.
3. Discuss the following points for each person:
    - What was the need that prompted _____'s call?
    - What were their qualifications?
    - How were they chosen?
    - When did they live?
    - What did God call them to do or proclaim?
    - What injustice was going on in the world at the time?
4. Together, discuss the following:
    - Has the community called you? In what ways?
    - How is the need for "witnesses" to Christ a compelling reason to call persons to ministry?
5. Conclude by noting what injustices are occurring in our neighborhoods, cities, country, or world today. How are we called to speak and act upon these issues?

Genesis 12:1–9 (Abram and Sarai)

Genesis 46:1–4 (Jacob)

Exodus 3:1–19 (Moses)

Esther 4:13–17 (Esther)

1 Samuel 3:1–19 (Samuel)

Jeremiah 1:4–19 (Jeremiah)

Ezekiel 1:3; 2:1–3 (Ezekiel)

Jonah 1:1–17 (Jonah)

Luke 1:26–56 (Mary)

Luke 10:38–42 (Mary and Martha)

John 1:35–51 (disciples)

Acts 9:1–19 (Saul/Paul)

How did Harriet Tubman, Absalom Jones, Richard Allen, Sojourner Truth, William Wilberforce, Abraham Lincoln, Martin Luther King, Marian Anderson, Rosa Parks, the Tuskegee Airmen, and the Buffalo Soldiers answer God's call?

- Do you think someone encouraged them to "answer the call"?
- Do you think you have been called by God to do something?
- Did you answer?
- Did you need help?
- Have you ever helped someone answer a call?

MUSIC

Hymn Sing

Negro spirituals expressed both faith and protest. Slaves were not allowed to speak their native tongue and were converted to Christianity. Their spirituals reflect both the hardship of slavery and biblical teachings, especially teachings on themes of deliverance. Many spirituals contained "code language" that gave advice on escaping, finding the Underground Railroad, and individuals who were sympathetic to their plight.

The spiritual "Wade in the Water" was a code to let escaping slaves know to wade in the water where their footprints could not be seen or dogs could not smell them. "Follow the Drinking Gourd" told slaves to watch for the North Star and always keep it before them as they escaped to Canada. As many slaves could not read, the spirituals gave them a way to express their faith and the repetitive structure of the music made it easy to sing. Invite someone to play the piano or other instrument to accompany the singing.

Since the words to many spirituals are already familiar, and many have repetitive choruses that even the youngest of participants can quickly learn, sing together some classic songs of both faith and protest. *Lift Every Voice and Sing II: An African-American Hymnal* (LEVAS) is a hymnal published by the Episcopal Church that contains many spirituals and contemporary hymns honoring Absalom Jones, Martin Luther King Jr., and other African-American saints of the church.

- "Wade in the Water" #143
- "Swing Low, Sweet Chariot" #18
- "Steal Away" #103
- "We Shall Overcome" #227
- "Go Down, Moses" #228

The song "Holy God, You Raise Up Prophets," #792 in *Wonder, Love, and Praise*,[3] is a powerful hymn by Harold T. Lewis and Carl

---

3. *Wonder, Love, and Praise: A Supplement to the Hymnal 1982* (New York: Church Publishing, 1997).

Haywood that specifically honors Dr. King and his work. Others in this hymnal:

- "Guide My Feet Lord" #819
- "I Want Jesus to Walk with Me" #805
- "It's Me, It's Me, It's Me, O Lord" #797

You can also find others online:

- "Follow the Drinking Gourd"—*http://www.followthedrinking gourd.org*
- "Michael Row the Boat Ashore"—*https://www.thoughtco.com /michael-row-the-boat-ashore-traditional-1322506*

DRAMA

Oratory Contest

Dr. King was known for his oratory skill and preaching. Invite group members to participate in a "Martin Luther King Jr. Oratory Contest." These can be based on quotes (see below) or on suggested topics, such as:

- What Freedom Means to Me
- How Can I Honor Those Who Have Gone Before Me by Promoting Justice
- I Have a Dream

Directions

1. Ask volunteers to choose a topic and prepare a speech of no more than five hundred words.
2. Provide a venue in which the speeches can be given, perhaps at a Martin Luther King Jr. celebratory dinner.
3. Award prizes for the best essays with donations to the person's favorite justice-focused charity.

Or

1. Invite individuals to give a presentation based on the following individuals and a quotation from them. Children may like to draw illustrations for each person or quote:
   - Harriet Tubman: "I started with this idea in my head. There's two things I've got a right to—death or liberty."
   - Sojourner Truth: "I have been forty years a slave and forty years free, and would be here forty years more to have equal

rights for all. I suppose I am kept here because something remains for me to do. I suppose I am yet to help break the chain."

- Marian Anderson: "If you have a purpose in which you can believe, there's no end to the amount of things you can accomplish."
- Rosa Parks: "I believe we are here on the planet Earth to live, grow up, and do what we can to make this world a better place for all people to enjoy freedom."
- Martin Luther King Jr.: "We must use time creatively, and forever realize that the time is always ripe to do right."

2. Engage in discussion about the prophetic words each shared.

- Of these five quotes, which is your favorite? Why?
- What is God calling you to do to respect the dignity of every human being and to love your neighbor as yourself?

FAITH IN ACTION

Standing on the Shoulders of Others

Many people have worked for civil rights and freedoms. They all were working for the respect and dignity of every human being, to reflect the unconditional love of God in Jesus. Since then, many others have followed in their footsteps, "standing on the shoulders of another" . . . and another . . . and another.

Read the following stories and prayers of others who shared in the struggle for equal rights. Then discuss the concluding questions and determine next steps.

> *Absalom Jones* was born a slave and learned to read by reading the Bible. *Richard Allen* bought his own freedom in 1784. Together they worshipped at the Methodist Church in Philadelphia where their presence in the congregation, along with many blacks, did not cause any notice until one Sunday in 1786 when the ushers came up and tapped both men on the shoulders while they were praying and informed them that they were required to sit in the balcony from this time forward. They didn't even let the men finish their prayers. Jones and Allen, along with other black worshippers. left the church that Sunday. Jones went to the Episcopal bishop of Philadelphia, the Rt. Rev. William White, and explained the situation. White agreed to allow the men to form an Episcopal Church with Jones serving as a lay reader. After a period of study he would be ordained. Allen did not like this plan as he wanted to remain in the Methodist Church, which he did so for a number of years. Allen then left the Methodist Church and formed the African Methodist Episcopal (AME) Church. Both men are probably the first blacks formally ordained in the United States. Absalom Jones is honored in the Episcopal calendar on February 23.
>
>> Set us free, heavenly Father, from every bond of prejudice and fear; that, honoring the steadfast courage of your servant Absalom Jones, we may show forth in our lives the

reconciling love and true freedom of the children of God, which you have given us in your Son our Savior Jesus Christ, who lives and reigns with you and the Holy Spirit, one God, now and forever. *Amen.*

—Prayer for Absalom Jones,
Lesser Feasts and Fasts, p. 160

William Wilberforce worked tirelessly to stop the slave trade coming from Africa through Liverpool, England, on the way to the United States. The stirring hymn "Amazing Grace" is his witness to this horrible practice and his faith journey.

Harriet Tubman, born a slave, was grievously injured by a slave owner and then escaped. Her head injury came at a time when Tubman was becoming deeply religious. Rejecting the scripture that said that slaves should be obedient, she found her guidance from the Old Testament stories of deliverance. She considered her trances—and the ensuing visions and dreams—times of God talking to her and directing her to help free slaves. She worked tirelessly for many years going back into "slave territory" to help slaves escape to Canada to freedom. The Underground Railroad was a pipeline for slaves to escape. Many white people along the route from Maryland to Canada assisted in this effort. Quilts with secret code designs were hung on clotheslines that served as maps to Canada. Using the North Star as their guiding point, many slaves travelled at night, led by Harriet Tubman who gained the nickname "Moses" as she guided slaves to the "Promised Land." Harriet was never caught and later became involved in the Civil War leading a Union raid—the first woman to do so. She was instrumental in the freedom of over seven hundred slaves.

Jesus, we praise you for your amazing daughter Harriet, who is rightfully called "The Moses of her People" for her work in the Underground Railroad. Although she suffered brutality that left her physically disabled, she still dared to escape. We praise you for Harriet's courageous efforts to free her people from slavery. We recall that she saved 756 slaves on one momentous occasion and, during the American Civil War, she managed her military intelligence missions so effectively that she gained the respect of generals. Harriet is so much larger than life, it's hard to imagine asking for the kind of inner strength she had. Yet violence still abounds in our world, and so we ask for the ingenuity and daring to risk our very selves as Harriet did to save our sisters and brothers from brutality. For we pray in the name of Jesus, who was beaten and humiliated, and yet died and rose to new life. *Amen.*

—"A Prayer for Harriet Tubman" from
She Who Prays, A Woman's Interfaith Prayer Book, p. 125

Sojourner Truth was born Isabella Baumfree, a slave in Dutch-speaking Ulster County, New York, in 1797. She was bought and sold four times, and subjected to harsh physical labor and violent punishments. She eventually ran away, and an abolitionist family purchased her freedom. In 1843, she declared that the Spirit called on her to preach the truth, renaming herself Sojourner Truth. As an itinerant preacher, Truth met abolitionists William Lloyd Garrison and Frederick Douglass. Garrison's anti-slavery organization encouraged Truth to give speeches about the evils of slavery. She never learned to read or write, but dictated what would become her autobiography—*The Narrative of Sojourner Truth*—in 1850. Truth survived on sales of the book, which also brought her national recognition. In 1851, Truth began a lecture tour that included a women's rights conference in Akron, Ohio, where she delivered her famous "Ain't I a Woman?" speech. In it, she challenged prevailing notions of racial and gender inferiority and inequality by reminding listeners of her combined strength (Truth was nearly six feet tall) and female status.

> Holy Comforter, we praise you for Sojourner's great faith in you, instilled by her own mother. We deplore slavery itself and the violence they and other slaves endured. We praise you for calling Sojourner out of bondage and for strengthening her in the fight against slavery and in the struggle for rights for all women. This magnificent woman's gifts for preaching and getting to the heart of the matter were unequalled. Her trust in you through years of extreme physical and emotional abuse challenges us to hold tight to you and to act, despite our fears, when we are called. We especially praise you that Sojourner had the independence of mind to ask you for an entirely new name, and that she made the most of being a strong woman, equal to, or better than, many a man. Help us claim our strengths and independence as we work with those in need. In the name of the Mother Spirit who empowered Sojourner and who empowers us, we pray. *Amen.*
>
> —Sojourner Truth, Evangelist, Abolitionist,
> Women's Rights, Orator, 1883, from
> *She Who Prays, A Woman's Interfaith Prayer Book*, p. 150

Rosa Parks was a lady who was simply too tired to go to the back of the bus and took the first available seat and would not get up to give the seat to a white person. This became the start of the Montgomery Bus Boycott. She worked tirelessly with Dr. Martin Luther King Jr.

> Lord God, we praise you for your daughter, Rosa, and for her courage in refusing to give up her seat on a segregated bus. Her "small action" became one of the sparks that started the Civil Rights Movement. We thank you that the woman had the will to let her case be used to

fight segregation laws in court. She worked to obtain black voting rights in Alabama and for civil rights throughout her life. When our actions have dire consequences, help us be as courageous as Rosa and her colleagues were and recall the good that ultimately came from their courage. *Amen.*

—Rosa Parks, one of the sparks of the Civil Rights Movement in 1955, Montgomery, Alabama, from *She Who Prays, A Woman's Interfaith Prayer Book*, p. 151

Ruby Bridges was the first black student at an all-white school in New Orleans. She was so young and afraid that she didn't realize that she was the only child in the school room that day. In *The Story of Ruby Bridges*, author Robert Coles shares how this extraordinary six-year-old helped shape history and was given courage through what she had learned from her grandmother: pray for your enemies.

The Tuskegee Airmen, the popular name of a group of African-American pilots who fought in World War II, were the first African-American military aviators in the United States. The military was still segregated at the time of World War II and these airmen suffered discrimination and were not allowed to fight. Despite many adversities they gained the right to fly and did so with distinction. They never served in combat but they served as bomber escorts in Europe. They were also known as the "Red-Tail Angels." On March 29, 2007, President George W. Bush awarded the Congressional Gold Medal collectively to approximately 300 Tuskegee Airmen or their widows. More than 180 airmen attended the January 20, 2009 inauguration of President Barack Obama.

Buffalo Soldiers supposedly originated with the Cheyenne warriors in the winter of 1877. Some say the Native Americans called the black cavalry troops "buffalo soldiers" because of their dark curly hair. It became a generic name for all African-American soldiers and is now used for U.S. Army units that trace their direct lineage back to the 9th and 10th Cavalry units whose service earned them an honored place in U.S. history. Buffalo Soldiers also served in the Spanish-American War, the Civil War, and helped keep the peace with the Native Americans. They further worked as park rangers in Yosemite and other national parks before the National Park Service was created. They helped make the "ranger hat" or "Smokey the Bear hat" famous.

Marian Anderson, famous mezzo soprano, encountered racism throughout her career. She was far better received on her numerous trips to Europe than in her home country, the United States. In 1939 she wanted to sing at Constitution Hall in Washington, D.C. The manager of the hall said that no dates were available. So instead, her manager arranged for her to sing on the steps of the Lincoln Memorial on Easter Sunday. Seventy-five thousand people enjoyed her concert. People were outraged, many musicians protested, and First Lady Eleanor Roosevelt resigned from the Daughters of the American Revolution (the owners of Constitution Hall).

Concluding questions

- Who do you know that could be added to this list?
- What is the most singular characteristic of these people?
- Who would you most like to have lunch with?
- What issues of social justice need to be addressed in your community? What steps need to be taken to begin to speak out and call for change?
- Develop a plan of action for moving forward, naming tasks to be accomplished and dates to begin the ongoing work.

Letter from a Birmingham Jail

Martin Luther King Jr. was arrested on April 12, 1963 for breaking an unjust law against political demonstrations in Birmingham, Alabama. He was held for twenty-four hours without being allowed his constitutional right to contact a lawyer. When he was allowed contact, he received a copy of the *Birmingham Post Herald* of April 13, which carried a public letter from eight local clergymen—Protestant, Catholic, and Jewish—calling the demonstrations "unwise and untimely." While the clergymen opposed segregation, they urged patience. Dr. King decided he might as well write back to let them know what was on his mind. His "letter to the editor," subsequently published in *Why We Can't Wait*,[4] was his response. In the letter he argues that he and his fellow demonstrators have a duty to fight for justice.

He addressed each of their statements, inferences, and assumptions, and also laid out his own disappointments with and vision for the church as an agent of God's justice and peace. This "Letter from Birmingham Jail" was rapidly picked up by media around the world and was immediately recognized as a document of historic significance. It has stood since as a landmark in the literature of social justice, exhibiting the same spirit as that of the great prophet Micah (6:8): ". . . what does the Lord require of you but to do justice, and to love kindness, and to walk humbly with your God?"

Together read and discuss Dr. King's letter. Choose any of the following questions to begin your conversation of how you can be part of the "beloved community" that Dr. King envisioned.

1. Dr. King explains the four steps of nonviolent protest: (1) fact finding, (2) negotiation, (3) self-purification, and (4) direct action. What do these mean to you?

---

4. Martin Luther King Jr., *Why We Can't Wait* (New York: Harper & Row, 1964), 77–100. See *https://swap.stanford.edu/20141218230016/http://mlk-kpp01.stanford.edu/kingweb/popular%5 Frequests/frequentdocs/birmingham.pdf.*

2. How have you experienced interdependence today and what did you learn from the experience?

3. What are the signs of persistent racism today?

4. What work remains to eradicate race prejudice and institutional racism in the United States? What specific issues present opportunities to make progress on this work?

5. Why is it important to the future of our nation that citizens have more than a distant and superficial knowledge of the civil rights struggle?

6. How might we change our personal attitudes and our institutions to protect human dignity?

7. Is racism a cause or a symptom of the widening economic disparity in the United States and why?

8. Do you agree or disagree that the wounds of racism and segregation in the United States extend to all Americans? How so?

9. What is your personal recollection or understanding of the civil rights era and how has it impacted your life?

10. What responsibility do people of faith have to actively work to correct the sin of racism? Specifically, what is being done in our churches to continue promoting personal and social transformation?

WORSHIP

Closing Prayers

You may ask for prayers from those present or prompt prayers by saying a phrase and then allow time for silent petitions to come from the group.

> In peace let us pray to the Lord, saying: *Lord have mercy.*
>
> For Martin our brother, for the faithful witness he gave.
>
> *Lord have mercy.*
>
> For Martin's advocacy for peace.
>
> *Lord have mercy.*
>
> For Martin's eloquent words that stirred the hearts of many.
>
> *Lord have mercy.*
>
> For those on whose shoulders we stand, Martin, Absalom, Sojourner, Ruby, Rosa, Harriet.
>
> *Lord have mercy.*
>
> For those who will stand on our shoulders.
>
> *Lord have mercy.*
>
> We pray for help as we do our part to treat others with dignity and respect. *Lord have mercy.*
>
> Hear our prayers O Lord. *Amen*

Sing: "There is a Balm in Gilead" one of Dr. King's favorite hymns (#203 in *Lift Every Voice and Sing II*)

Chapter 3

SUPER BOWL SUNDAY

INTRODUCTION

> Do you not know that in a race the runners all compete, but only
> one receives the prize? Run in such a way that you may win it.
> Athletes exercise self-control in all things; they do it to receive a
> perishable wreath, but we an imperishable one. So I do not run
> aimlessly, nor do I box as though beating the air . . .
>
> —1 Corinthians 9:24–26

While it's a bit of a stretch to think that Paul was speaking of
the Super Bowl as he addressed the Corinthian believers in these
verses—indeed, we recognize that he was drawing an analogy
between the athletic life and the life of faith—it's undeniable that
of all nonreligious "events" in American life, Super Bowl Sunday is one that has an enormous impact not only on our culture,
but also on the church. How many of us have looked around the
congregation on the morning of the Super Bowl and thought
to ourselves, "Yup, I can think of at least a dozen families that
would normally be here but are home getting ready . . . cleaning off their wide-screen TVs, moving the furniture around, and
preparing snacks." Did you know that, next to Thanksgiving,
Super Bowl Sunday is the next major "food consumption day" in
the United States? It's as close to being a national holiday as a
non-official holiday can be.

Why a Celebration for Super Bowl Sunday?

As Christians, we are a part of our culture, not separate from it. Just as we observe significant days in the Church year, our families, neighborhoods, friends, and churches recognize and—to varying degrees—also observe significant days in the secular year, days like New Year's Day, Valentine's Day, Mother's Day, and Father's Day. Super Bowl Sunday falls into this category as well, and provides an opportunity to acknowledge that, for a variety of reasons (some healthy, some perhaps not), this day impacts us too and provides a unique opportunity to explore a host of themes that we may seldom, in a spiritual context, take time to discuss, for example:

- Who are our heroes? Whom do we idolize and why?
- What is the role of sports in the life of our community? in our spiritual lives?
- When is competition healthy? When is it not?
- What makes a winner? a loser?
- When is cooperation the higher value? How about "trying your best"?
- What do sports say to us about our loyalties? our priorities? our goals?

In this celebration, your family and faith community will have the opportunity, not only to gather to watch the Super Bowl together, but also to engage in activities and discussions that explore a number of these significant topics.

A Brief History

For fans, detractors, and those indifferent to football, the history of the Super Bowl provides some interesting insight into the history of twenty-first-century America. Football itself evolved in the late nineteenth century, a hybrid of goal and kicking games imported from Europe. The first official game of intercollegiate football was probably played between Rutgers University and Princeton University on November 6, 1869.

The popularity of collegiate football increased rapidly during the first half of the twentieth century and dominated the football scene, although the origins of professional football actually date back to the late 1800s as well. In 1892, William "Pudge" Heffelfinger was the first person to be paid to play football for an athletic club. The first professional football league was formed in 1903 and the first "championship" game played in 1919. The next year the American Professional Football Association was formed, which became the National Football League the following year.

Initially, professional football found greatest acceptance in the Midwest, but its popularity spread quickly across the country, especially catching on after the 1958 NFL Championship Game, a contest nicknamed the "Greatest Game Ever Played." Within two years, a rival league formed—the American Football League. The two leagues started talking about a merger in the mid-1960s. Kansas City Chiefs' owner Lamar Hunt, who had been watching his children play with the Super Ball toy, called the first championship game played between the two top league teams the "Super Bowl." As it happened, the name stuck, though it didn't become official until the third annual game.

It was after Super Bowl IV in New Orleans in 1969 that the two leagues merged, dividing into two conferences, the American Football Conference and the National Football Conference. Today, the AFC and NFC champions meet each year in the Super Bowl.

The Super Bowl is the final game of each year's NFL playoffs. As the playing season kept expanding, so too the game kept being moved later in the year; originally played in mid-January, it now is played on the first Sunday of February.

Really? A Super Bowl Sunday Gathering at Church?

Is there any part of our life together as a community of faith not worth celebrating? And why not claim the Super Bowl for God as well? Besides the opportunities for opening up worthwhile discussions on a variety of related topics, you'll also be creating a deepened sense of fellowship . . . and make room for everyone, whether they are sports minded or not. You'll also honor those for whom football is a very big deal . . . and they are in your congregation.

Tips for Leaders

The core of this celebration is the gathering of your faith community to watch the Super Bowl itself. If your church has a projection system and TV connection, plan on projecting the game on the large screen in a meeting hall or even your sanctuary. If not, you might want to have several volunteers bring in their wide-screen (and hence lighter weight) TVs. Make sure to test all connections well beforehand.

If you are able to set up in a larger space, then various stations for the other activities found in this celebration could be set up around the periphery of the room. You'll also need an area designated for snacks and beverages. We further, as you'll see below, suggest one or more films that could be viewed by younger children and even youth or adults who aren't particularly interested in watching the game. You'll need separate spaces to show these as well, along with TVs for streaming or DVD players.

WORSHIP

Opening Prayer

Begin your session with one or both of these prayers.

Dear God, you have created us in your image and given us bodies to use for the spread of your Word throughout the world; we thank you for the gifts of strength, coordination, perseverance, and patience; help us to use our gifts for the good of others and not our own glory, to compete fairly respecting the skills and dignity of our fellow athletes, and to not boast in our own abilities but to celebrate the gifts of all; all this we ask through the your Son, Jesus Christ. *Amen.*

Generous God, you have given us talents and skills that we can use to the betterment of others, your creation, and ourselves. You have created us to strive for the best, and have set us at tasks that demand the best of us. Grant to all athletes, coaches, and fans the strength and courage to pursue excellence and fairness during this event. Give them the wisdom to play for their team and not just for themselves. We pray for the safety of these athletes; protect them from injury and harm. Give us a sense of enjoyment and community as we enjoy this time together, and bless the food that we will receive and bless the hands that have prepared it. All this we ask through your Son our savior Jesus Christ. *Amen.*

FOOTBALL PARTY

> So, whether you eat or drink, or whatever you do, do everything for the glory of God.
>
> —1 Corinthians 10:31

It can be argued that the Super Bowl is the premier sports event in the United States today. Parties abound from neighborhoods to family living rooms to restaurants and bars. The celebrations are for a favorite team, a great sports competition, state-of-the art commercials, and just a good reason to get together with friends and family.

However you choose to observe this event, remember to keep the focus on fellowship, building community, and recognizing the sacred in play and fun. Whether this will be one church-wide event held at the church or several events in various homes, the suggestions below and throughout this celebration can help people have a great afternoon or evening together.

Big Game Day parties feature as much conversation and fellowship as they do game watching. And this great conversation happens as people move from room to room in a house, or to different corners of a large room at your church. Take advantage of people's natural inclination to visit and talk, and focus your menu planning on "moveable foods"—foods that are easily eaten with the fingers and can be eaten while standing up or sitting on the couch. Be sure to include foods that children and teens will like too. Some football-themed recipes can be found on pages 84–85 which a variety of ages can make during the event, or share the recipes in advance for families to bring. Also invite participants to bring their favorite "football" recipes.

Advance preparation

- Decorate the space. Here are two suggestions:

  ○ Paint white lines on green paper tablecloths so they look like a football field. If you are using green cloth tablecloths, use white duct tape (or medical adhesive tape) for marking off the yardage.

- ○ One of the activities suggested (page 68) is to design "shields" for favorite sports teams or players. These can be hung around the community space for decoration when completed.

- Determine a room or space where craft activities will take place. Game watchers will appreciate if these are not in the same room as the big screen.

- Designate areas for quiet conversation and storytelling for those who need a break from watching the game.

CRAFTS

Team (or Athlete) Shields

> Whatever your task, put yourselves into it, as done for the Lord and not your masters, since you know that from the Lord you will receive the inheritance as your reward; you serve the Lord Christ.
>
> —Colossians 3:23–24

Participants can create shields for their favorite teams or sports figure, or use their imagination to create shields for themselves or someone else they consider to be courageous, athletic, or gifted.

Materials

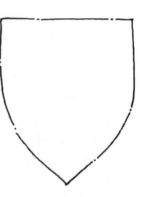

- poster board
- shield pattern, 1 per participant
- pencils
- markers (or tempera paint and brushes)
- scissors
- rulers

Directions

1. Invite everyone to create a shield using their favorite team's colors and mascot or to use their imaginations to create their own personal shields, including qualities that they believe make them courageous, athletic, or gifted. They could also create a shield for someone else they admire. (For example, St. Sebastian's shield [coat of arms] is divided into two parts. The left side has seven red crosses on a white background. The right side has three white arrows arranged on pale blue.)

2. Provide one sheet of poster board per participant to draw a shield shape on. Show the shield pattern noted here, or cut out shields in advance (which will be most helpful for younger participants).

3. Divide the shield into segments—usually two, three, or four parts.

4. Draw symbols onto each segment in pencil. Color them in with markers or tempera paint.

Note: Examples of shields and designs can be found here:

- *https://cassidybros.com/gate-of-heaven/shields/*
- *http://www.yourchildlearns.com/herald_inst.htm*
- *Saints, Signs, and Symbols: The Symbolic Language of Christian Art, 3rd edition,* by Hilarie and James Cornwell (Morehouse, 2009)

Football Facemask

Materials

- 2 plain, white paper plates (per person)
- crayons, markers, or paint (with brushes)
- tape
- scissors
- *optional:* elastic cord or string

Directions

1. Draw a face in the center of one paper plate.
2. Color the top edge and sides whatever color you want the football helmet to be.
3. Take the other paper plate and draw and cut out a football helmet facemask.
4. Tape the facemask you cut out onto the bottom half of the paper plate you colored, and you have a football player in their helmet.
5. Variation: Cut out the eyes, and attach string or elastic so that the mask can be worn by the child who made it.

Cheerleader Pom-Poms

Make pom-poms to go with your cheers (page 73) or for watching the Big Game.

Materials

- plastic grocery-type bags (3 per pom-pom)
- scissors
- heavy-duty tape: packaging, masking, or duct tape

Directions

1. Take three plastic bags and cut off the bottom edge.
2. Lay the bags on top of each other.
3. Take the tape and wrap it tightly around the three bags just below the handles.
4. With scissors, cut down the bags to make fringe. Now you have a pom-pom!

STORYTELLING AND BIBLE STUDY

Book Corner

Designate an area for quiet reading (or read-aloud sessions) with a rug, pillows to sit on, and baskets of picture books about sports for young children. Visit your local library to borrow titles. Possible suggestions:

- *Football with Dad* (*Little Golden Book*) by Frank Berrios
- *And Nobody Got Hurt! The World's Weirdest, Wackiest True Sports Stories* by Len Berman and Kent Gamble
- *And Nobody Got Hurt! 2: The World's Weirdest, Wackiest True Sports Stories* by Len Berman and Kent Gamble
- *A Very Special Athlete* by Dale Bachman Flynn
- *Goodnight Football* by Michael Dahl
- *My First Football Book* by the editors of Sports Illustrated
- *My Football Book* by Gail Gibbons
- *Nicky Jones and the Roaring Rhinos* by Lois G. Grambling
- *T Is for Touchdown: A Football Alphabet* by Brad Herzog
- *The Everything Kids' Football Book* by Greg Jacobs
- *What Is an Athlete?* by Barbara Lehn
- *Messi: The Rise to Stardom* by Roy Brandon
- *Stephen Curry: The Boy Who Never Gave Up* by Anthony Curcio

Champions Bible Study

The Bible is full of stories of individuals who served as champions in the name of God. This activity takes the themes of the characteristics that a champion for God may have.

Materials
- Bibles
- whiteboard, flip chart, or poster board with markers

Directions

- Within the group, read several of the great Bible stories of "champions":
  - Samson: Judges 13:2—16:31
  - David (and the story of slaying Goliath): 1 Samuel 17:4–51
  - Rahab: Joshua 2
  - Deborah: Judges 4–5
  - Moses: Exodus 3–15
  - Samuel (who was a boy at the time of this story): 1 Samuel 3
  - Mary (Jesus' mother, who had a lot of guts to say "yes" to the angel to be the mother of Jesus): Luke 1–2

- Make a list of the characteristics of each of these champions. Together discuss:
  - Do any of them share common attributes?
  - What made them different?
  - How did they perceive their call from God to do what they did?
  - Which "champion" do you relate to the most, and why?
  - Who in our culture today (sports, world leaders, people in the news, etc.) has these same attributes?

- Read Hebrews 11:1–39, often called the "faith" chapter, which could also be called the "champion" chapter. It is a great listing of people who did remarkable things. How do these individuals compare to the list of people and attributes we talked about earlier?

DRAMA

Three Cheers!

Rejoice in the Lord always; again I will say, Rejoice.

—Philippians 4:4

In small groups, devise a cheer for your team (or church or family). Think about actions—jumping, forming shapes with bodies, etc. As the Big Game is about to begin (or halftime), have each team share their cheer to the whole group. Make some cheerleader pom-poms to use with your cheer if you want (see page 70).

Use one of the following or write your own cheer:

Clap your hands (clap hands
    three times).
Stomp your feet (stomp feet
    three times).
Clap your hands (clap hands
    three times).
Stomp your feet (stomp feet
    three times).
We're the [church? team? fam-
    ily? other?] that can't be beat!
(Repeat as many times as you
    want.)

I'm a [animal? mascot? family
    member?] from [community?
    church? family?]
and only a [animal? natural
    disaster?] can knock me
    down.
If you don't like my apples, don't
    shake my tree
'cause I'm a [animal? mascot?
    family name?]!
Don't mess with me!

Get down, get funky, get loose
and shake your caboose!
Now start with the feet
Go feet 2, 3, 4
Go knees 2, 3, 4
Go hips 2, 3, 4
Go shoulders 2, 3, 4
Go head 2, 3, 4
Get down, get funky, get loose
and shake your caboose!

Ladies and gents
We present to all
a mighty fine team
That plays uh uh football
Hands up
rut tut tut tut
hands down
rut tut tut tut
all around
rut tut tut tut
to the ground
rut tut tut tut
uh rut tut!!

GAMES

Super Bowl Football Tossing Contest

Have nothing to do with profane myths and old wives' tales. Train yourself in godliness, for while physical training is of some value, godliness is valuable in every way, holding promise for both the present life and the life to come.

—1 Timothy 4:7–8

Even the littlest contestants can try their tossing skills with this multi-age, family-friendly game.

Materials

- for outdoors:
  - regular football—regulation size for older participants, miniature football for smaller children
  - goal posts erected at the end of the yard, moved closer for younger children
- for indoors:
  - foam (for example, Nerf®) football
  - hula hoop or basket for the goal

Directions

1. Give everyone a chance to score a goal by throwing the ball into the goal. It might be a good idea to break players into age groups, depending on the variety of ages participating.
2. The player in each age category who wins is the one who makes the target most of the time out of five attempts.

Football "Hot Potato"

This is a variation of the classic "Hot Potato." Ages participating must be able to catch. Play this game during one of the commercials during the Super Bowl game.

Materials

- soft Nerf® football

Directions

1. Gather everyone in a circle.

2. Instruct everyone to pass the ball to the person on their right as fast as they can, going around the circle continuously.

3. The person left holding the ball when the commercial ends gets to refill the snack bowls.

Super Bingo

All ages will enjoy a game of Super Bingo throughout the celebration. As people hear specific words during the Super Bowl game, they color in the squares.

Materials

- Bingo Card Templates, 1 per participant (download at *www.churchpublishing.org/faithfulcelebrations4*)
- crayons or highlighters, 1 per participant
- simple, themed prizes (candy, miniature footballs or helmets, etc.)

Directions

1. Create a unique bingo card for each attendee by randomly writing words from the following list in a different order on each card.

2. Use additional sports words of your own choosing . . . or possibly words likely to be used in advertising. You could also add the names of the teams in the game or some of their players.

3. Have crayons available for people to color in or mark the square when they hear the word.

4. Have simple, themed prizes available for those who win for a full row of horizontal, diagonal, vertical, and four corner squares.

Suggested words

touchdown	field	delay of game
first down	goal posts	extra point
field goal	injury	end zone
line judge	time out	facemask
referee	halftime	Hail Mary pass
instant replay	quarter	out of bounds
quarterback	second half	man in motion
safety	first half	line of scrimmage
interception	halftime show	nose tackle
fumble	season record	pass interference
helmet	blitz	punt
fans	ball carrier	off sides kick
NFL	clipping	playoffs
lost yards	coin toss	regular season
running back	cornerback	third and long
defensive end	dead ball	

Football Finger Flick Game

Remember playing this game in school? Folding up a piece of paper and "flicking" it through the goal was a simple game to play between classes, in the cafeteria, or at other times.

Materials

- 2 strips of copy paper or other heavy paper (not newsprint), cut into approximately 2" wide strips
- Popsicle® (or craft) sticks
- crayons, paints, or markers
- scissors or X-Acto® knife
- glue

Advance preparation

- Each strip of paper is going to be folded into a hard triangular shape, which is going to be the "ball." Take either bottom corner and fold it over to the other side. Keep folding up the strip of paper to the end; tuck the remaining paper inside the triangle.
- Each of the little triangle "balls" can be colored with the two Super Bowl teams' colors.
- You'll need 3 Popsicle/craft sticks, two for the sides of the end "posts" and one at the bottom to stabilize.
- Cut off the rounded ends to make them smooth and square to glue.
- Glue the sticks together to make an "end zone."
- Two "end zones" can be made and also painted to represent the teams.

Directions

1. Form two teams to represent the two Super Bowl contenders.
2. Each team member will take a turn trying to score a goal by "flicking" the triangular "ball" with their first or middle finger to send it through the goal posts.
3. The team with the most players to score a goal(s) at the end of a designated time wins.

Athletic Scripture Games

> And in the case of an athlete, no one is crowned without competing according to the rules.
>
> —2 Timothy 2:5

Many people are unaware that many of the principles that apply to athletics actually originated in the Bible. It might be fun to play some active games in which everyone can learn some words and phrases associated with athletics that can be found in scripture.

After the word or phrase is discovered, the person who has acted out ("Charades") or drawn it ("Win, Lose, or Draw") can share its application to our lives today.

Materials

- words or phrases (scriptural principles noted on pages 79–80) written out on small pieces of paper, including the explanations (Tip: you can download these *at www.churchpublishing.org /faithfulcelebrations4*), print and cut apart the individual words/ phrases/explanations, and place them in a basket or jar.
- timer (watch with second hand, egg timer, timer app on a cell phone, etc.)
- whiteboard, flip chart, newsprint, or poster board (for keeping score and/or drawing)
- markers
- basket or jar

Directions

1. Place papers in a basket or jar.
2. Review procedure and rules for the game chosen.
3. Divide into small groups, with each group choosing someone to be a timekeeper.
4. Explain the categories and their "signal":

    - Scriptural principles (pointer finger to forehead)
    - Sport mentioned in the Bible (palms up as if holding an open book)
    - Sports-related trait (bend one arm and squeeze your muscle with the other hand)

5. Taking turns, each team has one person draw a slip of paper out of the basket or jar and has 30 seconds to determine how they are to have their team guess the word or phrase correctly.

6. The individual then acts out (without words) or draws (without using numbers or letters) the word or phrase with the team shouting out answers.

7. The opposite team keeps time, with a 3- to 5-minute time limit.

Scriptural Principles

Don't bury your talents. In Matthew 25:14–30, Jesus shares the parable of the talents with his disciples. The key learning is that we are not to bury our "talents" but to utilize them to the best of our abilities. This is true in athletics and in our service to God as well.

Be a leader. In 2 Chronicles 31:21, Hezekiah was admired for pouring his entire heart and soul into his work. Hezekiah is an example for us both in athletics and in our service to God. Whatever your sport, you want to pour your entire heart and soul into your efforts. This will enable you to be a leader on your team, on the court, and on the playing field.

Stay in the moment. Paul encourages the Christians of Philippi in Philippians 4:4–8 to "stay in the moment." In verse 8 he encourages us to focus on purity and what is good. It is easy to lose focus in an athletic event, especially if the opposing team has scored or made a significant gain. It is important to stay focused on the task at hand and to "win the next play." All too often we see a team lose focus if they are behind, and fail to play up to the best of their abilities when they are behind. It is important to put past failures behind you and stay focused on the present to maximize your potential as an athlete and a servant to the Lord.

Leave "IT" in the gym or on the field. In athletics we are encouraged to "leave it in the gym or on the field." Great athletes will use every ounce of energy they have to win the game, event, or championship. Frequently after Olympic running events you will see athletes collapse from exhaustion. They have poured every ounce of energy into the race to the point they have "left it all on the field." Paul encourages the Corinthians in 1 Corinthians 9:24 to run the race so that they may obtain the prize knowing that only one runner will be crowned champion. To be successful in athletics and in life we have to "run the race."

Be prepared to endure. Paul tells Timothy in 2 Timothy 2:1–3, 12 to be prepared to endure hardship. Anyone that has participated in intercollegiate football or basketball has endured weeks of grueling practice sessions. Coaches put their teams through a period of difficult preparation in an effort to prepare them physically, mentally, and emotionally for the challenges that lie ahead. As athletes and followers of Christ, we must prepare ourselves to endure the challenges we will face as well.

Remember your priorities. All too often we see athletes lose focus on what is important in life (family, God, commitments). Paul encouraged the Colossians in Colossians 3:1–3 to focus on what is important in life. It is important in athletics as well as in our lives to maintain our focus on our relationship with our Lord and Savior, Jesus Christ.

Sports Mentioned in the Bible

- *Wrestling:* Genesis tells us that Jacob wrestled all night with a messenger of God.
- *Boxing:* In 2 Timothy, Paul tells us that he has fought the good fight.
- *Track:* In 2 Timothy, Paul says he has finished the race and kept the faith.
- *Fishing* was the occupation of most of the twelve apostles. Matthew 4:19: "Follow me, and I will make you fish for people."
- *Sailing* is a sport today, but boats were important modes of transportation in biblical times. Jesus and his apostles sailed on the Sea of Galilee.
- *Rowing* is a sport for many people today. In Acts 27, Paul traveled in sailboats and suffered in a shipwreck. When the sailing

vessels got close to shore, the passengers often traveled to the shore in dinghies or rowboats.

- *Swimming* saved the lives of some of those who suffered shipwreck with Paul, but today it is a very enjoyable sport.
- *Horseback riding*—a sport today—is referred to in 1 Kings.
- *Archery* also receives mention in 1 Kings.
- *Camping* is mentioned several times in the Old Testament, and in 2 Corinthians our earthly dwelling is referred to as a tent.
- *Mountain climbing:* Moses, of course, climbed Mount Sinai, and Jesus, Peter, James, and John climbed a high mountain where Jesus' transfiguration took place.
- *Walking* considerable distances is mentioned throughout the Bible, Abraham and Sarah being one example. Jesus met two disciples when they were walking on the road to Emmaus.
- *Javelin throwing*, a sport today, was an ancient method of warfare. Look for this in the Old Testament.
- *Discus throwing:* Was shooting a rock from a slingshot, the method of warfare in which David killed Goliath, somewhat similar to the throwing of a discus?
- *Baseball:* Did you know that baseball is mentioned in the Bible? You can find references in Genesis 1:1 and John 1:1: "In the big inning. . . ."

Sports-Related Traits

- *Endurance:* See Galatians 9:9.
- *Perseverance:* See James 1:2–4, Romans 5:3–5, and Hebrews 10:36.
- *Training:* See Ephesians 6:4.
- *Pursuit of the goal:* See Philippians 3:14.
- *Strength:* See Philippians 4:13 and Job 17:9.
- *Losing:* See Luke 9:25.
- *Physical training:* See 1 Timothy 4:8.
- *Spur others on:* See Hebrews 10:24.

FAITH IN ACTION

Make it a "Souper Bowl" Sunday

A simple prayer, "Lord, even as we enjoy the Super Bowl football game, help us be mindful of those who are without a bowl of soup to eat," is inspiring a youth-led movement to help hungry and hurting people around the world.

This prayer, delivered by Brad Smith, then a seminary intern serving at Spring Valley Presbyterian Church in Columbia, South Carolina, gave birth to an idea. Why not use Super Bowl weekend, a time when people come together for football and fun, to also unify the nation for a higher good: collecting dollars and canned food for the needy? Youth could collect donations at their schools and churches in soup pots, and then send every dollar directly to a local charity of their choice. The senior-high youth of Spring Valley Presbyterian liked the idea so much they decided to invite other area churches to join the team. Twenty-two Columbia churches participated that first year, reporting their results so a total could be determined, and then sending all $5,700 they had raised to area nonprofits.

That was 1990. Since then, ordinary young people have generated an extraordinary $100 million for soup kitchens, food banks, and other charities in communities across the country. In addition, hundreds of thousands of youth have experienced for themselves the joy and satisfaction of giving and serving, inspiring people of all ages to follow their generous example. Today the "Souper Bowl of Caring" is a national movement of young people working to fight hunger and poverty in their own communities around the time of the Super Bowl football game.

Make part of your Super Bowl celebration a time to remember those who may not have a place to gather with friends, watch the game on TV, or share in a banquet of snacks and festive food. In the weeks leading up to or on Super Bowl Sunday, young people take up a collection (many use a soup pot), asking for one dollar or one item of food for people in need. They give one hundred percent of their donation directly to the local hunger-relief charity of their choice. This can be your local food pantry, soup kitchen, or homeless shelter.

You can learn more about how you can participate at *www. souperbowl.org.*

RECIPES

Football Mini Subs

Ingredients

- meatballs (*Note: Buy these prepared—fresh or frozen—or make your own before the celebration.*)
- spaghetti sauce
- shredded cheese
- individual-size rolls

Directions

1. To make a batch, first shape each meatball into a mini football before cooking. (Obviously, if using frozen, pre-formed meatballs, give them time to properly thaw first.)
2. Cook the meatballs.
3. Add the cooked meatballs to a skillet of spaghetti sauce and warm them through.
4. For each sub, cut a V-shaped notch into the top of an individual-size roll, place a meatball or two in the roll, and top with cheese. You can lay the cheese across the football like the laces on a real football if you're feeling creative!
5. Finally, get the sandwiches in a huddle on a cookie sheet and place them in a warm oven for a few minutes to melt the cheese.
6. Just before serving, top with additional spaghetti sauce.

Mini Cheesecakes

Ingredients

- 1 16.5-ounce package refrigerated cookie dough of any kind
- 2 8-ounce packages cream cheese, softened
- 1 14-ounce can sweetened condensed milk
- 2 large eggs

- 2 teaspoons vanilla extract
- 1 21-ounce can cherry pie filling

Supplies

- 2 cupcake/muffin tins and paper liners (enough for 24 mini cheesecakes)
- oven

Directions

1. Preheat oven to 325°F. Line the muffin tin/cups with the paper liners.
2. Place one piece of cookie dough in each muffin cup.
3. Bake for 10 to 12 minutes, or until cookie has spread to the edge of the cup.
4. Remove from oven and cool.
5. With a mixer, beat together the cream cheese, sweetened condensed milk, eggs, and vanilla extract in a medium bowl until smooth.
6. Pour about 3 tablespoons of this cream cheese mixture over each cookie crust in the muffin tins.
7. Bake for an additional 15 to 18 minutes, or until set.
8. Cool completely in pan on a wire rack.
9. Top with pie filling.
10. Refrigerate for 1 hour before serving.

Note: This recipe makes 24 servings.

WORSHIP

Closing Prayer

A Sports Litany[1]

We pray for athletes, young and old . . .
*who develop important values such as loyalty, perseverance,
friendship, and sharing when playing sports and games.*

We pray for coaches . . .
*who appreciate the gifts of all players and have respect for the game,
place players before winning, and value sportsmanship.*

We pray for parents . . .
who love their children for who they are, not for how they perform.

We pray for fans . . .
who cheer their teams on with encouragement and support.

We pray for officials . . .
*who inspire fair play and protect the integrity of the competition,
athletes, and the game.*

O God, we pray for all who participate in games and athletics:
May their hearts be open to see your presence in and through
sports; may their minds remember the element of fun reflec-
tive of your Spirit; may their bodies reflect the gracefulness and
wonder of your creation. Let all who compete be enriched by
your presence on the course, in the gym, on the field, and on the
track. *Amen.*

---

1. Adapted from the Archdiocese of Seattle Department of Athletics, Office for Youth & Young
Adult Evangelization.

Chapter 4

VALENTINE'S DAY

INTRODUCTION

Create in me a clean heart, O God,
> and put a new and right spirit within me.
> > —Psalm 51:10

Ah, Valentine's, the season of love! Or, depending on your relationship status at the time, the season of annoyance! With a marketing push that plays runner-up to Halloween and Christmas, the commercial emphasis of Valentine's Day (now become an entire season) pressures us to be happy, in love, and share our hearts with someone special. Decorations go up in stores, schools, and homes. Whether we welcome it or feel it's forced upon us—candy hearts, massive card displays, boxes of chocolates, and all—the basic questions remain: What does all this Valentine's Day hype say to our children? What's the message from a faith perspective?

Some may be surprised to learn that the commemoration of St. Valentine is not included in the Church year (although Catholics do include him in their list of saints). There remains, in fact, some confusion of who exactly St. Valentine was.

A Bit of History

The history of the Christian church includes several St. Valentines (perhaps as many as fourteen), all martyred by the Romans. The

Latin name *Valentinus*, Anglicized as Valentine, was a common name at the time. *Valentinus* means "strong, powerful."

Of the St. Valentine with whom we associate the date of February 14 we know little, except that he was buried in Rome on that date. Different traditions suggest different identities—perhaps a Roman priest, a bishop, or a non-clerical martyr. It may be that the date celebrates several martyrs of the same name.

The Valentine of which we know the most is St. Valentine the Presbyter, for whom a church was built in Rome, perhaps in the fourth century. However, this St. Valentine is not one of those associated with February 14. The Eastern Orthodox Church remembers him on July 6.

In any case, none of these Valentines—whatever we do or do not know about them—has much to do with what has become the modern celebration of love known to us as St. Valentine's Day. For that we can thank fourteenth-century English author and poet Geoffrey Chaucer, who first associated the feast day of February 14 with romantic love in a poem titled "The Parliament of Fowls." In modern English, the line reads:

> *For this was St. Valentine's Day,*
> *when every bird cometh there to choose his mate.*

This reference stuck, picked up by other poets of the period and beyond. But why did Chaucer make this association? No one knows for sure: perhaps St. Valentine was, like so many of the martyrs, seen as embodying the ultimate example of love, the giving of life not only for the love of God, but for the love of other believers for whom such sacrifice would be a model. Or perhaps it's as simple as the fact that Chaucer's poem (an anniversary love poem) was ready to be read for the first time on February 14, and so he associated it with the saint remembered on that day.

A lovely but unsubstantiated legend tells us that one St. Valentine, on the night before he was to be martyred, wrote a card to a young woman whom he had healed, befriended, and with whom he had fallen in love. His card would, of course, have been the first "valentine."

Shakespeare, John Donne, and Edmund Spenser are all poets who reference St. Valentine's Day as a day of love. By the 1800s, the writing of valentines had become popular enough in England to spark their commercial production. As postal rates dropped, the sending of valentines increased. The practice caught on in the United States in the nineteenth century, and by the second half of the twentieth century had become the commercialized gift-giving celebration we're familiar with today. It's estimated that one-hundred-ninety million Valentines are exchanged each year in the United States alone. And now, of course, with our constant, widespread connection to the internet, add at least another fifteen million e-valentines to the estimate of those sent.

Valentine's Day and Faith

It is unlikely that not only the children of your faith community but also the youth and adults are observing Valentine's Day in one way or another, at home, at school, and/or at church. As mentioned earlier, it can be a fun day or a sad one. Some people outright oppose it, as they struggle with their own sense of loneliness or simply react negatively to its commercialization.

Your community of faith has the opportunity to reclaim this holiday as a "holy day," a day to celebrate love in all its facets; to acknowledge the beauty of human relationship; to express our gratitude for God's unbounded love for us; to allow people to express, as appropriate, their own frustration or hurt when it comes to relationships in general and Valentine's Day in particular; and perhaps, in all of this, to build greater bonds within your church family. It is with this understanding that this celebration is offered with the collection of activities that follow—from the baking and decorating of cookies, to imaginative games, to reflection on scripture, to the possibility of deep discussion on tough topics.

WORSHIP

Opening Prayer

Begin today's celebration with one of the following prayers, or another of your own choosing:

> God our Father,
> from the beginning,
> you have blessed creation with abundant life.
> Pour out your blessings upon us and all our relationships
> So that we may continue to grow in love and companionship
>   with each other
> And in holiness and faithfulness to you.
> We ask this through our Lord Jesus Christ your Son,
> who is alive and reigns with you,
> in the unity of the Holy Spirit,
> one God, now and forever. *Amen.*

> God of wonder and of joy:
> grace comes from you,
> and you alone are the source of life and love.
> Without you, we cannot please you;
> without your love, our deeds are worth nothing.
> Send your Holy Spirit,
> and pour into our hearts
> that most excellent gift of love,
> that we may worship you now
> with thankful hearts
> and serve you always with willing minds;
> through Jesus Christ our Lord. *Amen.*

VALENTINE'S WORSHIP SERVICE

Consider starting your celebration of Valentine's Day by worshiping the God of love. Sunday services are the principal act of worship of God. To honor Valentine's Day—and love—you can build special prayers or litanies into your Sunday worship. Or plan a special worship service, followed by a special dinner (see page 94) and/or congregational event that studies and celebrates love.

If you are planning a special worship service, a basic outline could be:

Gathering and Welcome

Opening Sentence: God is love, and those who abide in love abide in God, and God abides in them. —1 John 4:16

Opening Prayer (choose one):

> God of love, passionate and strong, tender and careful: watch over us and hold us all the days of our life; through Jesus Christ our Lord. *Amen.*

> Grant, we beseech thee, O Almighty God, that we who solemnize the festival of blessed Valentine, thy martyr, may, by his intercession, be delivered from all the evils that threaten us through Christ Our Lord. *Amen.* (Roman Catholic)

Hymn (select one or see page 115 for other choices):
- "Day by Day" (*The Hymnal 1982*, #654)
- "The King of Love my Shepherd Is" (*The Hymnal 1982*, #645)
- "What Wondrous Love is This" (*The Hymnal 1982*, #439)
- "God is Love, and where true love is God himself is there" (*The Hymnal 1982*, #577)

Readings (select one or more of the following suggestions):
- Old Testament
    - Genesis 29:15–28—Jacob falls in love with Rachel

- ○ Song of Solomon 2:10–13; 8:6, 7—Many waters cannot quench love
- Psalms
  - ○ Psalm 145:1–8
  - ○ Psalm 145:9–14
- New Testament
  - ○ 1 Corinthians 13—The greatest of these is love
  - ○ Ephesians 3:14—Rooted and grounded in love
  - ○ Colossians 3:12–17—Clothe yourselves with love
  - ○ 1 John 4:7–12—Let us love one another
- Gospel
  - ○ John 2:1–11—The wedding at Cana
  - ○ John 15:9–17—Greater love has no one than this

Intercessions:

Leader: We pray for the family of the Church, for loving relationships, and for the life of families around us.

People: Jesus, Lord of love, in your mercy, hear us.

Leader: Jesus, born in poverty and soon a refugee, be with families today who are poor and live in hunger and want . . .

People: Jesus, Lord of love, in your mercy, hear us.

Leader: Jesus, as you grew in wisdom and in favor with God and the people in the family of Joseph the carpenter, bring wisdom and the presence of God into the work and growth of families today . . .

People: Jesus, Lord of love, in your mercy, hear us.

Leader: Jesus, as you blessed marriage in the wedding at Cana, be with those preparing for marriage and with those who come to the end of their resources . . .

People: Jesus, Lord of love, in your mercy, hear us.

Leader: Jesus, as you healed Peter's mother-in-law, bring healing to those in our families who are ill today . . .

People: Jesus, Lord of love, in your mercy, hear us.

Leader: Jesus, when you were dying you called Mary and John to care for one another. Provide today for those who have lost their families: the bereaved and childless, orphans and widows . . .

People: Jesus, Lord of love, in your mercy, hear us.

Leader: Jesus, as you ate breakfast on the beach with your disciples after you were raised from the dead, bring the whole Church on earth and in heaven into your risen presence to eat at the eternal banquet.

People: Jesus, Lord of love, in your mercy, hear us, accept our prayers, and be with us always. *Amen.*

The Lord's Prayer

Hymn (select from those listed on page 91 or 115):

Blessing:

God the Holy Trinity make you strong in faith and love,
defend you on every side, and guide you in truth and peace;
and the blessing of God almighty,
the Father, the Son, and the Holy Spirit,
be among you and remain with you always. *Amen.*

AGAPÉ (LOVE) FEAST

The Christian duty to love one another has always been expressed in gatherings for fellowship. Such fellowship was realized from early times by participation in a common meal, and love feasts—*agapai*—are mentioned in Jude 12 and 2 Peter 2:13.

Among the Jews, meals for fellowship and brotherhood were common, and similar convivial gatherings took place among the Gentiles. It was natural that both Jewish and Gentile Christians should adopt such practices. The name agapé was later given to the fellowship meal. It is an anachronism, however, to apply it in its later sense to the conditions described in Acts and 1 Corinthians.

"The breaking of bread" referred to in Acts 2:42 and 2:46 may describe a common meal that included both agapé and Eucharist. Therefore, it would be appropriate to have a special meal as part of your festival gathering to celebrate Valentine's Day.

Decorate your dining area with hearts and flowers. Use pink, red, and white as your color theme on tablecloths, napkins, balloons, and centerpieces. During your celebration, create some of the foods to be shared, or invite participants to bring a portion of the meal to share.

Materials
- pink, red, and white tablecloths, napkins, balloons, and centerpieces
- drinks such as Love Potion Punch (see page 111)
- a nice main dish such as grilled salmon, steak, or pork roast
- rosemary roasted potatoes
- grilled fresh asparagus
- Caesar salad
- fresh breads
- red velvet cake and vanilla ice cream

Directions
1. Engage participants in decorating the room and the tables.
2. Place the food on a buffet or sit around the tables and eat family style.

CRAFTS

Beatitude Posters

The Beatitudes can set our hearts on the Reign of God. They are a way of life designed for those who want to live their lives to be a blessing. Beatitude people are kingdom people. They have a kingdom on their minds that won't let them rest until the whole world is striving to be just, compassionate, and single hearted. They call us forth from the cozy ruts of daily living and urge us to be Christ in the world. They tell us that the Reign of God is already in our midst if we can bless the world with Beatitude living. The Beatitudes are values that come straight from the heart of Christ.

"Blessed are the poor in spirit, for theirs is the kingdom of heaven.

"Blessed are those who mourn, for they will be comforted.

"Blessed are the meek, for they will inherit the earth.

"Blessed are those who hunger and thirst for righteousness, for they will be filled.

"Blessed are the merciful, for they will receive mercy.

"Blessed are the pure in heart, for they will see God.

"Blessed are the peacemakers, for they will be called children of God.

"Blessed are those who are persecuted for righteousness' sake, for theirs is the kingdom of heaven.

"Blessed are you when people revile you and persecute you and utter all kinds of evil against you falsely on my account. Rejoice and be glad, for your reward is great in heaven, for in the same way they persecuted the prophets who were before you."

—Matthew 5:3–11

In praying with these Beatitudes, try to imagine people who are poor and meek, those who are persecuted and hungry for justice and peace. Tell their story in words or pictures.

Materials
- white poster board or construction paper
- scissors
- markers or crayons
- magazines
- newspapers
- glue or glue sticks

Directions
1. Groups or individuals choose one of the Beatitudes to illustrate.
2. Cut out pictures and words from magazines and newspapers that exemplify the Beatitude.
3. Arrange and glue them onto paper or poster board, adding words or drawn illustrations.
4. Use for display in the gathering area of your celebration or share them if you will be having a closing liturgy as part of the reflection time.

Love Beads

Materials
- 25" length of red yarn, 1 per person
- plastic straws, cut into 1" pieces
- cellophane tape
- 2" heart cut out of construction paper with a hole punched in the center of it, 1 per person

Directions
1. Wrap a piece of tape around both ends of the yarn to make it easier for stringing.
2. String heart onto the yarn until it reaches the center of the length.
3. On either end of the yarn, string pieces of straw until 1"–2" remain.
4. Tie the two ends together and voilà, a necklace!

Make Valentines

The customs of Valentine's Day today come from the ancient Roman festival called *Lupercalia*, which took place on February 15. The festival honored Pan, the Roman god of nature, and Juno, the goddess of women and marriage. During this festival, young people drew names from a box and exchanged gifts.

Sending cards gradually replaced the custom of giving gifts. Today Valentine's Day, celebrated on February 14, is a time to display love and affection. People send cards, candy, or flowers as valentines to their sweethearts, friends, and family. Using the following materials, make valentines to give to the elderly or ill members of your congregation, or deliver them to a long-term-care facility, senior center, or hospital for distribution.

Materials

- red, white, and pink construction paper
- paper doilies
- glue
- stickers
- ribbon

- rickrack
- tissue paper
- glitter
- fabric scraps
- old Valentine's cards for cutting up
- paper arrows
- paper cupids
- lace
- pictures from magazines
- paper hearts
- feathers
- felt-tip markers
- "God is Love" written on small slips of paper for gluing onto the cards, 1 per person

Directions

1. Invite participants to choose from a variety of the available materials to create Valentine's cards.
2. Explain that they can make cards for people they know or for people in the hospital, nursing homes, or hospices.
3. Collect and arrange the delivery of the cards. If possible, have some or all of the children with their family involved in the delivery; this will make the experience much richer and more memorable for them.

Scratch-Off Valentine Wishes

Materials

- concordances
- 3" x 5" cardstock or plain index cards
- envelopes
- pencils

- felt-tip pens
- scissors
- clear Con-Tact® paper (or other clear adhesive shelf liner)
- metallic acrylic paint
- dishwashing liquid
- small, flat paintbrushes
- pennies
- Bible verses

Directions

1. Look up the word "love" in a concordance, making a list of short biblical phrases where the word is used. (See suggestions below.)
2. Write the phrase "Love Is . . ." on the top of the card.

3. Cut a strip of Con-Tact® paper 2" x 4.5" long.
4. Draw three hearts across the bottom of the card.
5. Write a bit of scripture in each heart about love.
6. Peel Con-Tact® paper and adhere sticky side on top of hearts and scripture.

7. To make the scratch-off solution, mix two-parts metallic acrylic paint with one-part dishwashing liquid.

8. Using a small, flat paintbrush, apply a thin coat of the scratch-off solution onto the hearts that have been covered with the Con-Tact® paper and let dry for an hour. Repeat with a second coat, and add a third coat if your paint looks streaky.

9. Package the card with a new penny.

Scripture examples

- The Lord is slow to anger, and abounding in steadfast love —Numbers 14:18a
- He will love you and bless you. —Deuteronomy 7:13
- For his steadfast love endures forever. —1 Chronicles 16:34
- But love covers all offenses. —Proverbs 10:12
- How sweet is your love. —Song of Solomon 4:10
- Your love is like a morning cloud. —Hosea 6:4
- Love is patient. —1 Corinthians 13:4
- Love never ends. —1 Corinthians 13:8
- The fruit of the Spirit is love. —Galatians 5:22

Valentine Straws

Materials

- 1" construction paper hearts (pre-cut)
- plastic straws
- glue

Directions

1. Place a straw on one of the hearts, toward the top third of the straw.

2. Place the second heart on top of the first, gluing them together, so that the straw is between the two hearts. Allow enough of

the straw to fit into a glass without the heart falling into the beverage, but enough on top to be able to drink through.

3. Use them with the Valentine Milk Shake (see page 114 for the recipe).

Angel Messages in a Jar

> If I speak in the tongues of mortals and of angels, but do not have love, I am a noisy gong or a clanging cymbal.
>
> —1 Corinthians 13:1

Our angels are always bringing us messages of love from God. This fun activity makes a special gift for someone who might need a dose of "angel" inspiration. Valentine's Day, the holiday of love, brings to mind this most beloved Bible passage.

Materials

- construction paper or colorful card stock to make small angels (download a template at *www.churchpublishing.org /faithfulcelebrations4*)
- scissors
- glue
- colored pencils, markers, or crayons
- clean jar
- large paper doilies

- decorating items: tissue paper, lace, beads, glitter, ribbon, stickers, etc.
- fabric scraps
- yarn or ribbon
- potpourri or perfume spray

Directions

1. Provide a sheet of angels on card stock to cut out, 1 per participant; or provide angels pre-cut to the group.
2. Have each participant write on each of their angel cards a quality of an angel such as love, compassion, friendship, strength, grace, courage, healing, etc.
3. Have participants decorate angels with glitter, stickers, scent, etc.
4. Have participants decorate jars covers with fabric or doilies.
5. Fill the jar with decorated angels.
6. These can be given as a gift with an attached card of instructions to pass on the angel message to someone else to brighten their day.

STORYTELLING AND BIBLE STUDY

God Is Love Bible Study

Participants examine God's great love for us.

Materials

- Bibles or printouts of the scripture passages

Directions

1. The scripture readings listed below are but a few that look at God's love for us. Read all of them as a group or divide into small groups, choosing one passage each. Ask these questions for each passage:

   - What does this passage say about God?
   - What does it say about love?
   - What does it say about people?
   - Who do you think showed love in this story? How did they do it?
   - Who are you most like in the story?
   - How do you show "God is love"?

2. Re-gather and invite small groups to present what they have learned to others.

Readings

- Genesis 1:26–28a
- Leviticus 19:34
- Ruth 1:16–18
- Matthew 22:36–38
- John 13:34
- 1 Corinthians 13:1–13

It's All Greek to Me

Biblical scholars have wrestled over the translations and meanings of the word "love" in the Bible for many years. The problem is that there are at least four Greek words for love, but only one English word.

Perhaps the best example of this is Paul's famous passage on love in his First Letter to the Corinthians. Which type of love is Paul referring to? Here is a very brief overview:

- *Storge* refers to the natural affection parents have for their children.

- *Eros* is sexual or romantic love. It is not used in the New Testament.

- *Filia* is friendship, brotherly/sisterly love toward someone we really like. It can also mean "adoration." (Interestingly, it is the root of Philadelphia—the "city of brotherly love.")

- *Agapé* is unconditional love, the love God has for us. It is the deepest love, and is based on doing good things for another person. It is a caring love, a love that loves another person for who they are: themselves. The best example is the great commandment "Love your neighbor as yourself."

For those who enjoy etymology (the study of words), invite them to study the biblical roots (Hebrew and Greek) behind the word "love." Find some good commentaries, Bible dictionaries, and a concordance that will help guide the study. Consider checking out these two online sources:

- *www.textweek.com*
- *www.biblegateway.com*

Look up the word "love" in each resource. If you have a seminary in your community, invite one of the New Testament professors to lead a class for you. Another recommended book on the subject is *The Four Loves* by C.S. Lewis.

Directions

- After reviewing some of the information and resources listed above, discuss:
  - What are the Greek words for "love" and what is the difference between them?
  - What are examples of their use in the Bible?
  - What do these different words tell us about love, our love for each other, and God's love for us?
- What is one thing you have learned in this study that will inform your love for God's world in the future?
- Create a PowerPoint presentation with photographs (*www. bing.com/images*) and scripture to show the full depth and breadth of the meaning of the word "love" in scripture.
- Show the PowerPoint presentation during your Valentine's Day gathering, worship service, or as an ongoing slideshow for people to watch at their leisure. Add music if you'd like.

GAMES

Biblical Couples Concentration Game

This is a good way to help remember characters in Bible stories that go together. Cards for the game need to be made in advance, or part of the activity before playing could be the construction of the cards.

Materials

- blank index cards or cardstock
- markers
- *optional:* laminator or clear Con-Tact® paper

Directions for making the cards

1. On ten blank index cards (or 3" x 5" pieces of cardstock), write one of each of the names listed below (their "mate" is in parentheses next to it).
2. Add illustrations if desired, drawing a picture of each person using your imagination.
3. Laminate or cover with clear Con-Tact® paper to make them more permanent if desired.

Rebekah (Isaac)	Isaac (Rebekah)
Eve (Adam)	Adam (Eve)
Bathsheba (David)	David (Bathsheba)
Sarah (Abraham)	Abraham (Sarah)
Zipporah (Moses)	Moses (Zipporah)
Rachel (Jacob)	Jacob (Rachel)
Delilah (Samson)	Samson (Delilah)
Ruth (Boaz)	Boaz (Ruth)
Esther (Ahasuerus)	Ahasuerus (Esther)
Mary (Joseph)	Joseph (Mary)

Directions for playing the game

1. Shuffle the cards. Lay them face down in five rows of four.

2. One person at a time chooses two cards to turn over. If they make a pair (example: Abraham and Sarah), they keep the cards and go again.

3. If they do not match, they turn them back over, and the next person takes a turn.

4. Continue until all the pairs have been discovered and "captured" by the players.

5. The one with the most pairs wins the game.

Valentine's Day Bingo

Materials

- heart-shaped bingo cards made out of heavy construction paper in colors of pink, white, or red, 1 per participant (A template can be downloaded at *www.churchpublishing.org/ faithfulcelebrations4.*)

- small candies, such as Valentine's Day hearts, M&M'S®, or Red Hots® for space markers

- decorated Valentine's Day bag for holding call cards

Advance preparation

- Print the cards in advance with pictures on each square that represent Valentine's Day such as hearts, Cupid, friends hugging, a favorite cartoon character holding a heart, picture of a box of candy, pictures of miniature candy hearts with sayings on them, angels with a heart, etc. Clipart images can be found on the internet.

- In advance of the game, print out the pictures or names on 2" x 2" squares and cut them out to put in the Valentine's Day bag.

Directions

1. Choose someone to be the caller (children can take turns being a caller).
2. The caller picks a square (pictures for the younger children, names for the older children) and shows it to the group of players, describing it in words.
3. If they have the picture or word on their card, each participant puts a piece of candy on that square.
4. Have one free "blackout" space on each card so each player will automatically have one space covered.
5. The first child to get a compete row across, down, or diagonally wins.
6. Everyone can eat their playing pieces at the end.

FAITH IN ACTION

Healthy Heart Station

February is American Heart Month, sponsored by the American Heart Association. Sponsor a "healthy heart" station at your celebration. Tap into your local Red Cross (a doctor or nurse may also be a member of your congregation). This could feature blood pressure screening and other simple diagnostic tests that will help your community learn to be more health conscious.

As you open the Healthy Heart Station, you might begin with this prayer:

> O God, the author of salvation and giver of health, you have entrusted to your Church the healing ministry of your Son, Jesus: instill in us a passion to seek wholeness of mind, spirit, and body, give us confidence in the healing power of Christ, help us to be good stewards of our bodies, and give us a desire to promote health of persons in our congregation and community; through Jesus Christ our Lord. *Amen.*

Another option is to host a Health and Wellness Fair for your neighborhood or the community, as well as your church membership. This is a cost-effective way of providing valuable health information and screening services for many people at a single event. Successful health and wellness fairs require a good amount of planning, commitment, and dedication. Here is an example of some possible resources that may have local personnel who can offer a screening:

- American Cancer Society—*www.cancer.org*
- American Diabetes Association—*www.diabetes.org*
- American Heart Association—*www.heart.org*
- American Lung Association—*www.lung.org*
- Arthritis Foundation—*www.arthritis.org*
- National Cancer Institute (NCI)—*www.cancer.gov*

- National Diabetes Education Program—*www.niddk.nih.gov /health-information/communication-programs/ndep*
- National Eye Health Education Program—*https://nei.nih.gov /nehep*
- National Institute of Neurological Disorders and Stroke—*www.ninds.nih.gov*
- National Osteoporosis Foundation—*www.nof.org*
- Substance Abuse and Mental Health Services Administration (SAMHSA)—*www.samhsa.gov* (government agency that provides education on alcohol, drug abuse, and mental health)

RECIPES

Well, maybe not "Love Potion No. 9" (recorded in 1963 by The Searchers), but the recipes below say, "I care about you." You could serve them for the fellowship time after church on the Sunday closest to Valentine's Day, as part of your celebration, or at movie night.

Love Potion Punch

This recipe makes 12–15 cups. Double or triple the recipe as needed.

Ingredients

- 1 6-ounce can frozen orange juice, thawed
- 1 6-ounce can frozen pink lemonade, thawed
- 1 6-ounce can frozen limeade, thawed
- 4 cups cold water
- 1 large bottle (about 4 cups) ginger ale

Directions

1. Combine all ingredients except ginger ale.
2. Pour over ice cubes in punch bowl.
3. Add ginger ale just before serving.
4. Garnish glasses with a small strawberry or swizzle stick with a heart atop it.

White Chocolate Hearts

Ingredients

- 2½ cups all purpose flour
- ½ teaspoon baking soda
- ½ teaspoon baking powder
- 1 cup butter
- 1 cup sugar
- 2 tablespoons milk

- 1 egg
- 1 teaspoon vanilla
- 1 teaspoon red gel food coloring
- *optional:* 4 ounces white chocolate, melted

Supplies

- heart-shaped cookie cutter(s)
- electric mixer
- mixing bowl
- rolling pin
- oven
- cookie sheets
- pot holders or hot pads
- racks for cooling
- clean, flat surface for rolling out the dough

Directions

1. Sift together the dry ingredients and set aside.
2. With an electric mixer, cream the butter and sugar on medium-high until light and fluffy.
3. Add the milk, egg, vanilla, and food coloring, mixing on low just until blended.
4. Keeping the mixer on low, add the dry ingredients slowly, stopping the mixer once to scrape down the sides of the bowl. Mix until blended; do not overbeat.
5. You may chill the dough at this point, or proceed.
6. Taking one-third of the dough, place it on a well-floured surface and roll out until ⅛" thick.
7. Cut out heart-shaped cookies.
8. Place on a very lightly greased baking sheet, about ½ inch apart, and bake in a 350°F oven about 10 minutes or until lightly browned.

9. Continue until all the dough is used. It's okay to re-roll dough so that all of it gets used.

10. Cool on racks. Be certain cookies have cooled before eating.

Eat Your Heart Out

Chilling layers of gelatin and condensed milk easily assembles this lovely dessert. Even sweeter, it's low fat. With adult supervision, children can help mix the ingredients.

Ingredients

- 1 14-ounce can of sweetened condensed milk
- 3 3-ounce packages of red flavored gelatin
- 2 ¼-ounce envelopes of unflavored gelatin
- boiling water
- cold water

Supplies

- 9" x 13" glass pan
- refrigerator
- mixing bowl and spoons

Directions

1. Dissolve one package of flavored gelatin in ¾ cup boiling water. Add ¾ cup cold water, then pour the mixture into a 9" x 13" glass pan and refrigerate for 1 hour.

2. Stir together ½ cup boiling water and the condensed milk.

3. In a separate bowl, dissolve the unflavored gelatin in ½ cup cold water for 1–2 minutes.

4. Thoroughly mix in ¾ cup boiling water, then combine this mixture with the milk and let it cool.

5. Add half the mixture to the pan of red gelatin, pouring it over a spatula to slow the stream, and refrigerate for 20 minutes.

6. Continue alternating layers—gelatin mix, remaining milk mix, final gelatin mix—chilling each layer for 20–30 minutes to set it.

7. Create individual servings with a heart-shaped biscuit or cookie cutter.

Valentine Milk Shakes

Ingredients

- 10 ounces frozen strawberries (or raspberries or cherries)
- 4 cups cold milk

Supplies

- blender

Directions

1. Combine fruit and milk in blender.
2. Blend until smooth and frothy.
3. Pour into a glass. (Add a decorated straw—see page 100.)

WORSHIP

Closing Worship

Hymn:

Choose one or more of the following or another favorite from your tradition:

- "In Christ there is no East or West" (*The Hymnal 1982* #529)
- "God is Love" (*The Hymnal 1982* #576)
- "Jesu, Jesu" (*The Hymnal 1982* #602)
- "Where true charity and love abide, God is there" (*The Hymnal 1982* #606 or *Wonder, Love, and Praise* #831)
- "Love divine, all loves excelling" (*The Hymnal 1982* #657)

Litany:

Men and boys:	Blessed are the poor in spirit
Women and girls:	For theirs is the kingdom of heaven.
All:	Let us be a blessing to others.
Men and boys:	Blessed are those who mourn,
Women and girls:	For they shall be comforted.
All:	Let us be a blessing to others.
Men and boys:	Blessed are the meek,
Women and girls:	For they shall inherit the earth.
All:	Let us be a blessing to others.
Men and boys:	Blessed are those who hunger and thirst for righteousness,
Women and girls:	For they shall be satisfied.
All:	Let us be a blessing to others.
Men and boys:	Blessed are the merciful,
Women and girls:	For they shall obtain mercy.
All:	Let us be a blessing to others.
Men and boys:	Blessed are the pure in heart,

Women and girls: For they shall see God.

All: Let us be a blessing to others.

Men and boys: Blessed are the peacemakers,

Women and girls: For they shall be called sons and daughters
                      of God.

All: Let us be a blessing to others.

Men and boys: Blessed are those who are persecuted for
                      righteousness' sake,

Women and girls: For theirs is the kingdom of heaven.

All: Let us be a blessing to others.

Blessing: Creator God, make us strong in faith and love, defend us on every side, and guide us in truth and peace; and the blessing of God Almighty, the Father, the Son, and the Holy Spirit, be among us and remain with us always. *Amen.*

Chapter 5

SNOW DAYS

INTRODUCTION

In the Northern Hemisphere, winter begins in mid-December and ends in mid-March. During this season the days grow shorter, and the nights grow longer. The southern portion of the United States has mild winters characterized by warmer weather and rain instead of snow. Cold weather causes many changes in the environment: water freezes and forms ice, snow, sleet, and icicles. Most plants and animals become dormant and rest. People's lifestyles may also change; indoor activities, winter sports, and needing to adjust one's clothing to give protection from the elements affect most. And of course, inclement weather often means schools are closed.

John Updike writes in his essay "The Cold":

Cold is an absence, an absence of heat, and yet it feels like a presence—a vigorous, hostilely active presence in the air that presses upon your naked face and that makes your fingers and toes ache within their mittens and boots. Cold is always working, it seems—busy freezing water in the ponds and rivers, knitting intricate six-sided snowflakes by the billions, finding cracks around the walls and windows of your house, forcing furnaces in the cellar to roar away. Cold fights you—it doesn't want your automobile engine to ignite in the morning, and once your car is on the highway it clogs its path with snow and slush. A whole secondary world of dirt, of sand and salt, is called into being by the cold, and an expansive and troublesome array of wearing apparel—mufflers, earmuffs, wool-lined boots and gloves, parkas, leggings, long underwear, and knitted face-masks.[1]

How might you take a snow day (or any day in the winter) to gather and explore this season from a faith perspective, enjoying God's creation in traditional ways with a faithful spin?

Holding a Snow Day Celebration

Typically, "snow days" come when an unexpected storm brings heavy snowfall, below-freezing temperatures, or icy roads forcing the cancellation of schools and often office closings. For working parents this can be a hardship, having to find childcare for school-age children or staying home with them and forsaking the day's paycheck. Faith communities may wish to open up their churches to offer care provided by volunteers. If so, the activities within this celebration may offer ready-to-enact plans.

This may not be feasible, so what follows on these pages could be used in the home, gathering all the children from the neighborhood together for a day of fun. A day during a winter vacation for children to gather at your church could also be offered. For an intergenerational gathering, hold your celebration on a weekend afternoon when (if weather permits) activities can also be held outside (if there is snow). Typical outdoor snow activities can be offered with a twist and a spiritual theme:

- Mark an area of the snow with a stick for each participant or team. They can use the snow in that area to create a sculpture of a biblical character. After all the sculptures are created, have a "show and tell" to tell the story of each sculpture, with everyone moving from sculpture to sculpture to hear from its creators.

- Invite all ages to make snow angels. What fun it would be to have everyone laughing on the ground, waving arms and legs in the snow while singing, "Angels we have heard on high."

---

1. John Updike, "The Cold," in *More Matter: Essays and Criticism* (New York: Random House, 2000).

- Make snow people to line the sidewalks around your church or home. How could they offer a welcome to those who come to worship? (Think of Calvin's snow people from the cartoon strip "Calvin and Hobbes.")

Global Warming

On a more serious note, winter is a good time for congregations and families to reflect upon the changing weather patterns of this planet Earth, our island home. As the climate continues to change, the seasons are seeing a shift as well, with winters coming later and leaving earlier than ever recorded. Both the Bible Study and Faith in Action sections of this celebration offer some ideas for reflection on this topic.

Climate change is fueling an increase in the intensity and snowfall of winter storms. The atmosphere now holds more moisture, and that in turns drives heavier-than-normal precipitation, including heavier snowfall in the appropriate conditions. Heavy snowfall and snowstorm frequency have increased in many northern parts of the United States. The heavier-than-normal snowfalls recently observed in the Midwest and Northeast United States are consistent with climate model projections. In contrast, the South and lower Midwest saw reduced snowstorm frequency during the last century. Overall, snow cover has decreased in the Northern Hemisphere, due in part to higher temperatures that shorten the time snow spends on the ground. (Learn more at *www.climate communication.org.*)

Global warming is challenging winter sports across the globe, and scientists say the phenomena could slim the number of potential Olympic hosts dramatically in the future. Research published in January 2018 from the University of Waterloo[2] found that only eight of the twenty-one previous winter Olympic hosts would be able to do so again by 2100 without urgent action to address

---

2. *https://uwaterloo.ca/news/news/climate-change-will-limit-where-winter-olympics-can-be-held* (accessed March 1, 2018).

climate change. Average temperatures during the Olympics are up from around 33°F before the 1960s to 46°F this century, according to the study.

Many communities that depend on winter tourism are at risk. What happens, for instance, when there is not enough snow to support skiing? With a changing climate, will winter recreation-based economies still be sustainable? Although climate change happens slowly, community planners and natural resource managers need to understand how to best respond to changing environmental conditions. The sustainability of winter recreation destinations depends on decisions made today.

WORSHIP

Opening Prayer

Begin today's celebration with one of the following prayers, or another of your own choosing:

> O heavenly Father, who has filled the world with beauty: Open our eyes to behold your gracious hand in all your works; that, rejoicing in your whole creation, we may learn to serve you with gladness; for the sake of him through whom all things were made, your Son Jesus Christ our Lord. *Amen.*
>
> —"For Joy in God's Creation," Book of Common Prayer, p. 814

> Our Great and Caring God—creator, preserver, comforter. White beauty feathers out from every brown twig and blade. Yet in the cold deadness of winter, many of us are hibernating, untouched by the beauty, waiting for the warm aliveness of spring. Whenever our hours of self-absorption come, may our spirits rise to the recreative freshness of uniting with you. May we seek your glory in love and serving one another. May we will to put forth the effort it takes to understand each other. Through worshipping and working together, may we come to know our God and our neighbors more profoundly. In Christ's Name. *Amen.*
>
> —Afton Bitton, "Reawakening in January"
> from *Women's Uncommon Prayers*, pp. 45–46

A Winter's Prayer

Creator God at the start of this New Year when thoughts turn again to beginnings starting afresh

new leaves and turning skeletons free from cupboards:

Be with us.

As we gaze into the distance of fresh mission grounds of hopes and dreams, opportunities for service, challenges, and uncertainties:

Be with us.

Take our fears and turn them into strengths, take our lack of faith and empower us through the Spirit who breathes life into this world, whose presence is reflected in the icy chill of winter's breath as well as the comforting warmth of a summer breeze.

Be with us.

Walk with us into this New Year of opportunity.

Be with us.

—adapted from a prayer by John Birch[3]

---

3. *www.faithandworship.com/Prayers_Winter.htm#ixzz58WaiyuMY.*

CRAFTS

Winter Mitten Sun-Catcher

See, I have inscribed you on the palms of my hands; your walls are continually before me.

—Isaiah 49:16

The wintery colors of blue and white are captured in this fun and colorful project. Even the littlest hands can help paste the design. Hang this catcher at home or around your church's gathering spaces for a lovely window decoration all winter long.

Materials

- clear Con-Tact® paper
- light-blue construction paper
- tissue paper: light blue, blue, and lavender (or confetti)
- scissors
- silver ribbon
- white craft glue

Directions

1. Draw a simple pattern for a mitten. (Or trace the shape of participants' hands, fingers closed.)
2. Cut out two mittens from light-blue construction paper. Cut the centers of both mittens out also, making sure there is a border that remains all the way around each mitten, forming a frame of the mitten shape.
3. Cut tissue paper into small squares, similar to confetti.
4. Carefully peel off the back from a section of the Con-Tact® paper, only removing enough to cover one side of the mitten.
5. Place one of the mittens onto the clear adhesive paper, lining up the top of the mitten with the top of the Con-Tact® paper.

6. Place small squares of tissue paper onto the clear adhesive paper in the center of the mitten. Mix up the colors so that you do not have one color all in one place.

7. Add a small dab of glue to the top and bottom of the mitten that is on the Con-Tact® paper.

8. Cut a piece of silver ribbon for the hanger and fold in half. Place the two open ends of the ribbon at the top of the mitten in the dab of glue.

9. Take the other mitten half and carefully line it up with the mitten on the Con-Tact® paper. Gently press down onto the glue.

10. Gently peel back the clear adhesive paper backing and then fold over the top of the mitten creation to seal both sides. Press down and smooth out.

11. Use scissors to trim around the outside of the mitten.

Make Snow

Not all parts of the country get snow in the winter months. Some children may have not even experienced snow—so why not make some? This recipe for "snow dough" is soft and elastic and does not harden. Keep it covered in containers or plastic bags.

Materials

- Mixing bowl
- 6 cups of flour
- 1 cup of salad oil
- water
- large mixing spoon
- plastic zipper bags
- *optional:* smocks to protect clothing

Directions

1. Mix together the flour and salad oil in a bowl.
2. Add enough water to make the dough soft and pliable.
3. Instead of using a spoon to mix the dough, participants can knead and mix with their hands.
4. Create mini snow people, snowballs, or whatever is desired.

Indoor Ice Sculpture

Materials

- Blocks of ice (These can be purchased in advanced or you can make your own by freezing water in large containers or milk cartons with the tops cut off—plan enough time in advance to have enough frozen blocks for everyone.)
- coarse salt
- dishpans or other large containers
- spoons
- plastic knives
- small bowls
- water
- *optional:* eye droppers, food coloring

Directions

1. Place a block of ice in a dishpan.
2. Put a small bowl of coarse salt close by.
3. Put a small bowl of water close by.
4. Working in pairs (one child with an adult for example), spoon the salt on the ice. Wherever the salt touches the ice, the ice will melt faster, leaving a pattern of holes.
5. Using the salt and water, plus the plastic knives, begin to carve and shape the block of ice into a sculpture.

6. As an option, set out three eyedroppers and three small bowls filled with diluted red, yellow, and blue food coloring. The colors can be dropped onto the ice, and as it melts the colors will run together and produce secondary colors.

Milk Carton Bird Feeder

Create an easy feeder for the birds.

Materials

- empty half-gallon milk or juice cartons
- scissors or X-Acto® knife (adult use only)
- birdseed
- heavy string
- hole punch or ice pick (adult use only)

Directions

1. Using the X-Acto® knife, cut an opening in the side of the carton to make a large window.
2. Poke a hole in the center of the top of the carton where the seam lies.
3. Thread a length of string through the hole, forming a hanger.
4. Fill the carton up to the level of the opening with birdseed.
5. Bring the birdfeeder outside and hang in a tree or another suitable place.

STORYTELLING AND BIBLE STUDY

Environmental Bible Study

> As long as the earth endures, seedtime and harvest, cold and heat, summer and winter, day and night, shall not cease.

> —Genesis 8:22

The terms "ecological crisis" and "environmental problems" at heart refer to the troubled relationship between human beings and God's creation. As Stephen Jurovics writes, "At one end of that relationship are secular issues such as climate change, endangered species, and toxic wastes, and at the other end are biblical teachings about the interrelationships among God, people, and nature."[4] The first five books of the Hebrew scriptures offer numerous aspects of these interrelationships.

In all the seasons of the year we can see the effects of climate change. Winter is no different. A predominate view asserts that the rise in temperature on the globe is due in large part to the emissions of heat-trapping gases into the atmosphere due to fossil fuels which lead to a build up in carbon dioxide in our atmosphere. For Christians and Jews, we often turn to Genesis 1:28: "God blessed them, and God said to them, 'Be fruitful and multiply, and fill the earth and subdue it; and have dominion over the fish of the sea and birds of the air and over every living thing that moves upon the earth.'" What other verses and stories from scripture might we read to enlighten our views of how we care for the earth?

Below are a variety of scriptures to study in small groups or all together. Choose several and compare them, using the questions noted below to guide your conversation.

Scripture

- Genesis 1:28
- Genesis 7 in its entirety, but with a focus on 7:1–5

---

4. Stephen A. Jurovics, *Hospitable Planet: Faith, Action, and Climate Change* (New York: Morehouse, 2016), 3.

- Genesis 9 in its entirety, but with a focus on 9:1–3 and 9:15–17
- Leviticus 25:23, 26:3–12
- Psalm 24
- Matthew 5:17–19a
- Matthew 7:12

Scripture questions
- What is this verse saying to you?
- What is the human responsibility toward creation according to this verse?
- How do these scriptures differ from one another? Are there similarities?
- As people of faith, what are we called to do to maintain our part of the covenantal relationship with God?

Digging deeper
- How do you view the applicability of Genesis 7 to the goal of preserving global diversity?
- How does global warming contribute to the loss of species?
- To what degree do you see climate change as damaging God's creation?
- Is climate change a spiritual issue? Why or why not?

Next steps
- Refer to Faith in Action, page 132 to take this study further.

Reading Corner

Collect some children's story books focused on the theme of winter and place them in a basket surrounded by soft cushions and pillows for quiet reading.

- *The Snowy Day* by Ezra Jack Keats
- *David and the Ice Elf* by Winifred Morris

- *The Mystery of the Red Mitten* by Steven Kellogg
- *The Mitten* by Jan Brett
- *White Snow, Bright Snow* by Alvin Tresselt
- *Owl Moon* by Jane Yolen
- *Snowmen at Night* by Caralyn Buehner (There are many titles about what snowmen do in this series.)
- *Snowflake Bentley* by Jacqueline Briggs Martin
- *The Snowman* by Raymond Briggs
- *Stopping by Woods on a Snowy Evening* by Robert Frost, illustrated by Susan Jeffers
- *The Winter Solstice* by Ellen Jackson

DRAMA

Snowflakes in the Breeze

In an open space (inside or out), invite everyone to be a snowflake.

Materials

- CD player, digital device, or other means of sharing music loud enough for everyone to hear (especially if you are doing this outside)
- Music selections that have a variety of tempos (Classical pieces may work best.)

Directions

1. Invite everyone to stand a few feet apart from one another.
2. Turn on the music and invite participants to imagine themselves as a snowflake falling from the sky.

3. Gradually increase the tempo of the music, until everyone is twirling and spinning around as if driven by the wind.
4. Gradually decrease the music's tempo until the drifting snow finally comes to rest on the ground.
5. *Optional:* Play the familiar "Skater's Waltz" and pretend to skate around the room.

PRAYER ACTIVITY

Cotton Ball Snowflake Prayers

Make a winter scene of a "snow-filled" sky filled with prayers.

Materials

- large sheet of blue construction paper or blue butcher paper (like that used to cover bulletin boards)
- white cotton balls
- markers and/or crayons
- glue

Directions

1. Tape the large blue paper on a wall at a level all ages can reach.
2. With a marker, label the top of the paper in large letters: My Prayer for Winter
3. Invite participants to glue a cotton ball on the paper and write a prayer next to the "snowflake."
4. Fill the paper with prayers of thanks and prayers for others.
5. *Optional:* Someone could read aloud all the prayers at your closing gathering.

FAITH IN ACTION
Global Warming Study

Follow up your reading of Genesis 7–9 (see page 127) with a discussion of action steps. Use these questions[5] to determine where your focus may lie and what action you might take as an individual, family, or worshiping community.

1. Describe the covenant God makes with Noah and all life on earth and your thoughts about the inclusiveness of that covenant.

2. To what degree do you see climate change as damaging God's creation?

3. As people of faith, what are we called to do to maintain our part of the covenantal relationship with God?

Assisting the Homeless

> "For I was hungry and you gave me food, I was thirsty and you gave me something to drink, I was a stranger and you welcomed me, I was naked and you gave me clothing, I was sick and you took care of me, I was in prison and you visited me." Then the righteous will answer him, "Lord, when was it that we saw you hungry and gave you food, or thirsty and gave you something to drink? And when was it that we saw you a stranger and welcomed you, or naked and gave you clothing? And when was it that we saw you sick or in prison and visited you?" And the king will answer them, "Truly I tell you, just as you did it to one of the least of these who are members of my family, you did it to me."
>
> Matthew 25:35–40

Any time of year is difficult for those who live on the streets or in homeless shelters. Research the needs of the homeless in your

---

5. These questions are taken from Stephen Jurovics' book, *Hospitable Planet: Faith, Action, and Climate Change* (New York: Morehouse, 2016). This book might serve as a starting point for determining what action plans you might be called to explore and act upon.

community and learn the most appropriate response you can take to help those who may be cold, hungry, or shelterless.

- Conduct a gently used coat drive. Include boots, hats, gloves, and scarves, and consider all ages of men, women, and children.
- Consider the ministry of the Empowerment Plan. The EMPWR coat is a water-resistant jacket, which can transform into a sleeping bag or be worn as an over-the-shoulder bag when not in use. The coat is constructed of durable, water-resistant Cordura® fabric from Carhartt®, upcycled automotive insulation from General Motors, and other materials provided by generous donors. It costs $100 to sponsor a coat, which covers the cost of labor, materials, and overhead expenses. Learn more at *www.empowermentplan.org/the-coat*.
- Collect toiletries (like those you might receive when staying in a hotel such as shampoo, hand lotion, mouthwash, etc.), gift cards for coffee shops, packages of tissues or handkerchiefs, cough drops, lip balm, etc. Distribute them to those who are located on street corners or parks in your town or city asking for assistance.

RECIPES

Snow Cones

A summer treat can be made to share with others at your event as a frosty winter refreshment. Everyone will love it!

Supplies

- orange, apple, or grape juice frozen in ice cube trays
- paper cone cups
- ice cream scoop
- blender

Directions

1. Place cubes in a blender.
2. Start and stop several times until you have crushed ice.
3. Scoop into paper cone cups.

Note: Five frozen fruit cubes will equal about 1 serving.

Mitten Toast

Ingredients

- bread
- peanut butter and/or jelly (check for allergies)

Supplies

- toaster
- knives (plastic for children)

Directions

1. Cut slices of bread into mitten shapes.
2. Toast them in an oven or toaster.
3. Spread with peanut butter, jelly, or other spreadable food.

4. *Note:* Crusts and bread pieces can also be toasted in an oven and tossed outside for the birds.

Snowflake Macaroons

Ingredients

- 2 egg whites
- 1 cup rolled oats
- ⅓ cup of honey
- ½ cup grated coconut

Supplies

- mixing bowls
- mixing spoon
- electric mixer
- greased cookie sheet
- oven

Directions

1. Beat egg whites in a small bowl until stiff.
2. Combine warm honey and oats in another bowl.
3. Mix well. Add coconut.
4. Fold in egg whites.
5. Drop by the spoonful onto a lightly greased cookie sheet.
6. Bake at 300°F for 25 to 30 minutes.

WORSHIP

Closing Worship

Hymn:

Choose one or more of the following or another favorite from your tradition:

- Tis winter now, the fallen snow (*Church Hymnary*, 4th ed. #234)
- In the bleak mid winter (*The Hymnal 1982* #112)
- All things bright and beautiful (*The Hymnal 1982* #405)

Prayer:

A Winter Prayer

Let us huddle together this morning,
our community a place of warmth in our lives
as we share the flame of hope and connection.
Let us allow the frost of isolation and bitterness to melt away
as we open ourselves to a sense of peace and spirit.
We extend our thoughts to all those who are cold this morning,
lacking shelter or love to keep them warm.
Let us wrap our prayers around them and each other like
     scarves,
and wish each other safe journeys through the storm.
May we be insulated from fear as the earth is insulated by the
     snow,
And, like bulbs, may we continue to grow and open inside,
     despite the cold,
Ready for the spring, to stretch and grow towards justice. *Amen.*

—Kate Wilkinson[6]

---

6. *Used with permission. www.revkatewilkinson.com.*